ECCENTRICS

P9-COP-798

CRITICAL READING SERIES

ECCENTRICS

21 Stories of Unusual and Remarkable People—
with Exercises for Developing Critical Reading Skills

JAMESTOWN  PUBLISHERS

a division of NTC/CONTEMPORARY PUBLISHING GROUP
Lincolnwood, Illinois USA

copyright page

ISBN 0-89061-109-2

Published by Jamestown Publishers,
a division of NTC/Contemporary Publishing Group, Inc.
4255 West Touhy Avenue,
Lincolnwood (Chicago), Illinois 60712-1975, U.S.A.
© 1999 by NTC/Contemporary Publishing Group, Inc.
All rights reserved.
No part of this publication may be reproduced, stored in a retrieval
system, or transmitted in any form or by any means without the prior
written permission of the publisher.

10 11 12 13 024 12 11 10 09

CONTENTS

UNIT THREE

To the Student

Most people feel that it's fun to be one of the crowd, doing what everyone else is doing. They find comfort in knowing that they belong to a group whose rules and customs they all value. Unlike most people, however, the characters you will read about in this book made a habit of thinking and acting in their own unique styles. They refused to be limited by the rules of conventional life. For them, the thrill of living was found in breaking the mold society had fashioned for them.

Eccentrics force each of us to examine the reasons why we think and act as we do. They expand our choices in life by doing what we thought was impossible or unthinkable. Each lesson in this book will introduce you to a different person who lived by his or her own set of rules. The 21 articles focus on a wide variety of people—from playwrights to fire engine chasers, from professional pranksters to world-class shoppers. You are sure to find the stories of these unconventional characters both entertaining and thought-provoking.

All the articles tell about actual events and real people. As you read and enjoy them, you will also be developing your reading skills. *Eccentrics* is for students who already read fairly well but who want to read faster and to increase their understanding of what they read. If you complete the 21 lessons—reading the articles and completing the exercises—you will surely increase your reading speed and improve your reading comprehension and critical thinking skills. Also, because these exercises include items of the types often found on state and national tests, learning how to complete them will prepare you for tests you may have to take in the future.

How to Use This Book

About the Book. *Eccentrics* contains three units, each of which includes seven lessons. Each lesson begins with an article about an unusual event, person, or group. The article is followed by a group of four reading comprehension exercises and a set of three critical thinking exercises. The reading comprehension exercises will help you understand the article. The critical thinking exercises will help you think about what you have read and how it relates to your own experience.

At the end of the lesson, you will also have the opportunity to give your personal response to some aspect of the article and then to assess how well you understood what you read.

The Sample Lesson.   Working through the sample lesson, the first lesson in the book, with your class or group will demonstrate how a lesson is organized. The sample lesson explains how to complete the exercises and score your answers. The correct answers for the sample exercises and sample scores are printed in lighter type. In some cases, explanations of the correct answers are given. The explanations will help you understand how to think through these question types.

If you have any questions about how to complete the exercises or score them, this is the time to get the answers.

Working Through Each Lesson.   Begin each lesson by looking at the photographs and reading the captions. Before you read, predict what you think the article will be about. Then read the article.

Sometimes your teacher may decide to time your reading. Timing helps you keep track of and increase your reading speed. If you have been timed, enter your reading time in the box at the end of the lesson. Then use the Words-per-Minute Table to find your reading speed, and record your speed on the Reading Speed graph at the end of the unit.

Next complete the Reading Comprehension and Critical Thinking exercises. The directions for each exercise will tell you how to mark your answers. When you have finished all four Reading Comprehension exercises, use the answer key provided by your teacher to check your work. Follow the directions after each exercise to find your score. Record your Reading Comprehension scores on the graph at the end of each unit. Then check your answers to the Author's Approach, Summarizing and Paraphrasing, and Critical Thinking exercises. Fill in the Critical Thinking chart at the end of each unit with your evaluation of your work and comments about your progress.

At the end of each unit you will also complete a Compare/Contrast chart. The completed chart will help you see what the articles have in common. It will also give you an opportunity to explore your thoughts and opinions about these unusual people we call eccentrics.

SAMPLE
LESSON

ALVIN SHIPWRECK KELLY
A Lucky Fool

He "just went up for a breath of fresh air." At least that is what he claimed. But Alvin "Shipwreck" Kelly's idea of getting a little fresh air was rather offbeat. On November 17, 1927, Kelly and his pilot took off from Curtiss Field, on Long Island, in a biplane. Hundreds of curious spectators gathered near the runway to see Shipwreck Kelly try another bizarre stunt. Earlier that year, Kelly had gained fame by spending 12 days and 12 hours sitting atop a flagpole on the roof of the St. Francis Hotel in Newark, New Jersey.

2   This time, however, the most famous flagpole sitter in the United States had something else in mind. He planned to sit on a 10-foot iron pole fastened to the top wing of a biplane. As the plane made its first pass over the airfield, Kelly climbed out of the cockpit. Gingerly, he pulled himself onto the top wing. Then he wrapped himself around the pole and waved to the crowd below. On the second pass over the airfield, Kelly wagged his foot over the edge of the wing. Then he climbed up the pole and sat on a small crossbar attached near the top. When the

Shipwreck Kelly perched on a 65-foot flagpole, which was located at the top of the 15-story Times Square Hotel.

spectators saw him perched there on the third pass, they roared their approval. Shipwreck Kelly had pulled off another crowd-pleasing trick.

3   The 1920s were a fun-loving decade, filled with loony fads such as goldfish swallowing and marathon dancing. But the nuttiest craze of all was flagpole sitting. And the nuttiest flagpole sitter was Shipwreck Kelly. Kelly loved to court danger. He boasted that he had survived five sea disasters while serving in the navy in World War I. His experiences earned him the nickname "Shipwreck." He also claimed to have walked away from two airplane crashes, three automobile accidents, and a train wreck—all without getting a scratch.

4   Kelly billed himself as the "luckiest fool alive." No one disputed the claim. He certainly was foolish. And he was lucky to live at a time when people would actually pay to watch him sit on a flagpole. Kelly sat on many flagpoles, but he preferred those on hotel rooftops. The hotels were grateful for the attention he attracted. They gave him free lodging, meals, and a cash advance. In addition, Kelly earned part of the fee that the hotel charged people to sit on the roof and watch the spectacle.

5   Shipwreck Kelly loved publicity. He also loved to smash old notions about the

limits of human endurance. On June 21, 1930, Kelly climbed a 125-foot pole on the Steel Pier in Atlantic City. A disk about the size of a record album had been attached to the top. There Kelly made himself as comfortable as possible. He was

Kelly atop a 60-foot flagpole in 1942. Kelly hoped to enlist in the U.S. Navy at the end of his four days on this flagpole.

determined to break his own flagpole-sitting record of 23 days and seven hours. Kelly wanted to stay aloft for a full 28 days. That, he felt, would be a record no rival flagpole sitter would ever break.

6   For the next 28 days Kelly stayed on top of the pole. Thousands of people went by daily to witness the implausible stunt. They wondered how anyone could actually live on top of a flagpole day after day. But Kelly had all the details worked out. First of all, he devised a way to sleep without falling off. Before going to sleep, he would put his thumbs into small holes in the flagpole shaft. If he swayed while dozing, the twinge of pain in his thumbs caused him to right himself without waking. A hollow tube attached to the side of the pole served as his toilet. He even managed to bathe himself every now and then, with a sponge and a pail of water.

7   Shipwreck Kelly spent his time on the flagpole writing about his experience, listening to a radio, and reading his fan mail. He got about a hundred letters a day from admirers around the country. Kelly's wife and young child, Alvin, Jr., visited on Saturdays. They were hoisted up the pole in a special chair.

8   When Kelly finally reached his goal, everyone naturally expected him to come down. But Kelly must have been enjoying his life high above Atlantic City. He decided to stay put a little longer. A doctor checked him and pronounced him physically fit. Lack of exercise, however, was causing him to gain weight. To prevent any further weight gain, he cut back to just one meal a day.

9   At last, on the morning of August 9, Shipwreck Kelly let people know that he was coming down. He wanted to finish in style, so a barber was hoisted up to give him a haircut and a manicure. When Kelly finally descended the pole, twenty thousand screaming fans greeted him. It took him four minutes to slip down to the Steel Pier. When he hit the ground, he had trouble walking. After all, he hadn't taken a step since June 21. He had been aloft for 1,177 hours—more than 49 days. Shipwreck Kelly had broken his own record by more than 600 hours.

10   The Steel Pier stunt was the highlight of Kelly's flagpole-sitting career. Kelly continued to sit on flagpoles around the country for another five years. But the glory days of flagpole sitting had passed. Such exhibitions of human endurance no longer fascinated people. Shipwreck Kelly slowly faded into obscurity. He collapsed and died on a New York sidewalk in 1952. Tucked under his arm was a scrapbook filled with old newspaper clippings about the exploits of Alvin "Shipwreck" Kelly. 🍂

If you have been timed while reading this article, enter your reading time below. Then turn to the Words-per-Minute Table on page 71 and look up your reading speed (words per minute). Enter your reading speed on the graph on page 72.

Reading Time: Sample Lesson

_____ : _____
Minutes   Seconds

A Finding the Main Idea

One statement below expresses the main idea of the article. One statement is too general, or too broad. The other statement explains only part of the article; it is too narrow. Label the statements using the following key:

M—Main Idea   **B—Too Broad**   **N—Too Narrow**

___N___   1. To give the spectators a thrill, Shipwreck Kelly sat on a ten-foot iron pole fastened to the top wing of a biplane. [This statement is *too narrow*. It doesn't tell anything about Kelly's flagpole sitting.]

___B___   2. During the 1920s, many entertainers tried unique stunts to gain attention and to make money. [This statement is *too broad*. While true, the statement doesn't tell us anything about Shipwreck Kelly.]

___M___   3. Shipwreck Kelly, a determined publicity seeker, won national fame by setting flagpole-sitting records. [This statement is the *main idea*. It tells who Shipwreck Kelly was and what he did.]

___15___   Score 15 points for a correct M answer.

___10___   Score 5 points for each correct B or N answer.

___25___   **Total Score:** Finding the Main Idea

B Recalling Facts

How well do you remember the facts in the article? Put an X in the box next to the answer that correctly completes each statement about the article.

1. One of the loony fads of the 1920s was
   - ☐ a. tree climbing.
   - ☒ b. goldfish swallowing.
   - ☐ c. marathon road races.

2. Kelly earned his nickname while he
   - ☒ a. served in the navy.
   - ☐ b. sat on a flagpole in Atlantic City.
   - ☐ c. was still in grammar school.

3. Kelly preferred flagpoles situated
   - ☐ a. at baseball fields.
   - ☐ b. near government buildings.
   - ☒ c. on hotel rooftops.

4. Kelly set his all-time flagpole-sitting record at
   - ☒ a. Atlantic City.
   - ☐ b. Newark.
   - ☐ c. Curtiss Field.

5. When Kelly died, he was holding under his arm
   - ☐ a. a miniature flagpole.
   - ☐ b. a portable radio.
   - ☒ c. old newspaper clippings.

Score 5 points for each correct answer.

___25___   **Total Score:** Recalling Facts

C | Making Inferences

When you combine your own experience and information from a text to draw a conclusion that is not directly stated in that text, you are making an inference. Below are five statements that may or may not be inferences based on information in the article. Label the statements using the following key:

C—Correct Inference   F—Faulty Inference

_F_   1. Shipwreck Kelly enjoyed privacy more than most people do. [This is a *faulty* inference. He loved publicity and life in the limelight.]

_C_   2. Shipwreck Kelly was not afraid of heights. [This is a *correct* inference. No one afraid of heights would walk on the wing of a plane or sit for days on top of a flagpole.]

_C_   3. Kelly had a good sense of balance. [This is a *correct* inference. He needed a good sense of balance to sit for so long on the small disks he used on flagpoles and to take short naps without falling off.]

_F_   4. Kelly's wife was also a flagpole sitter. [This is a *faulty* inference. Kelly sat alone. His wife visited him once a week using a special chair.]

_F_   5. Kelly always came down from flagpoles when it started to rain. [This is a *faulty* inference. He had to expect some rain during his long stays on the tops of flagpoles, and he never cut his stays short because of rain.]

Score 5 points for each correct answer.

_25_   **Total Score:** Making Inferences

D | Using Words Precisely

Each numbered sentence below contains an underlined word or phrase from the article. Following the sentence are three definitions. One definition is closest to the meaning of the underlined word. One definition is opposite or nearly opposite. Label those two definitions using the following key. Do not label the remaining definition.

C—Closest   O—Opposite or Nearly Opposite

1. But Kelly's idea of getting a little fresh air was rather <u>offbeat</u>.

     _C_   a. unusual

     _____   b. not rhythmic

     _O_   c. common

2. The 1920s were a fun-loving decade, filled with <u>loony</u> fads such as goldfish swallowing and marathon dancing.

     _____   a. dangerous

     _O_   b. sensible

     _C_   c. extremely silly

3. Thousands of people went by daily to witness the <u>implausible</u> stunt.

     _O_   a. believable

     _C_   b. incredible

     _____   c. frightening

4. Shipwreck Kelly slowly faded into <u>obscurity</u>.

     _C_   a. forgotten state

     _____   b. retirement

     _O_   c. fame

5. Tucked under his arm was a scrapbook filled with old newspaper clippings about the <u>exploits</u> of Alvin "Shipwreck" Kelly.

___O___ a. boring deeds

_____ b. stupid ideas

___C___ c. daring acts

___15___ Score 3 points for each correct C answer.

___10___ Score 2 points for each correct O answer.

___25___ **Total Score:** Using Words Precisely

Enter the four total scores in the spaces below, and add them together to find your Reading Comprehension Score. Then record your score on the graph on page 73.

Score	Question Type	Sample Lesson
25	Finding the Main Idea	
25	Recalling Facts	
25	Making Inferences	
25	Using Words Precisely	
100	**Reading Comprehension Score**	

Author's Approach

Put an X in the box next to the correct answer.

1. What is the author's purpose in writing "Alvin 'Shipwreck' Kelly: A Lucky Fool"?
   ☐ a. To encourage the reader to take risks
   ☒ b. To inform the reader about Shipwreck Kelly and his crazy stunts
   ☐ c. To emphasize the similarities between the 1920s and the current decade

2. From the statement from the article "Tucked under his arm was a scrapbook filled with old newspaper clippings about the exploits of Alvin 'Shipwreck' Kelly," you can conclude that the author wants the reader to think that
   ☐ a. when Kelly died, he was still a popular figure.
   ☐ b. when Kelly died, he was writing a book about his career.
   ☒ c. when Kelly died, he was a sad, lonely man who longed for his old glory days.

3. What does the author imply by saying "And he was lucky to live at a time when people would actually pay to watch him sit on a flagpole"?
   ☒ a. People at other times wouldn't have paid to watch a flagpole sitter.
   ☐ b. People in the 1920s were very foolish.
   ☐ c. Shipwreck Kelly was lucky throughout his life.

4. Choose the statement below that best describes the author's position in paragraph 6.
   ☐ a. Kelly was crazy to sit on a flagpole for so long.
   ☐ b. Kelly was very casual about sitting on the flagpole in Atlantic City.
   ☒ c. Kelly was well prepared for the flagpole-sitting in Atlantic City.

___4___ Number of correct answers

Record your personal assessment of your work on the Critical Thinking Chart on page 74.

Summarizing and Paraphrasing

Put an X in the box next to the correct answer.

1. Below are summaries of the article. Choose the summary that says all the most important things about the article but in the fewest words.

   ☒ a. In the 1920s, Shipwreck Kelly was famous for his flagpole-sitting and other crazy stunts. When people lost interest in his exploits, however, he faded into obscurity.

   ☐ b. Shipwreck Kelly was a famous flagpole-sitter in the 1920s.

   ☐ c. Shipwreck Kelly gained fame for his flagpole-sitting in the 1920s. He set a record in Atlantic City by sitting atop a flagpole for more than 49 days. After that stunt, though, people lost interest in Kelly, and he died a forgotten man.

2. Read the statement about the article below. Then read the paraphrase of that statement. Choose the reason that best tells why the paraphrase does not say the same thing as the statement.

   Statement: Kelly was called "Shipwreck" because he claimed that he had survived five sea disasters while serving in the navy during World War I.

   Paraphrase: Kelly earned the nickname "Shipwreck" from his years in the navy.

   ☐ a. Paraphrase says too much.

   ☒ b. Paraphrase doesn't say enough.

   ☐ c. Paraphrase doesn't agree with the statement about the article.

3. Choose the best one-sentence paraphrase for the following sentence from the article:

   "He wanted to finish in style, so a barber was hoisted up to give him a haircut and a manicure."

   ☐ a. Kelly completed his stunt by giving a barber a haircut and manicure.

   ☐ b. According to the style of the times, Kelly completed his stunt by having a barber share the flagpole with him.

   ☒ c. Kelly wanted to complete his stunt with a flourish so he had a barber brought up to cut his hair and nails.

_____3_____ Number of correct answers

Record your personal assessment of your work on the Critical Thinking Chart on page 74.

Critical Thinking

Follow the directions provided for questions 1 and 3. Put an X in the box next to the correct answer for the other questions.

1. For each statement below, write O if it expresses an opinion and write F if it expresses a fact.

   ___F___ a. Kelly spent 12 days and 12 hours sitting on a flagpole in a hotel in Newark, New Jersey. [This statement is a *fact* because it can be proved.]

   ___O___ b. Shipwreck Kelly was the most daring man in the 1920s. [This statement is an *opinion;* it cannot be proved.]

   ___F___ c. Kelly died in 1952 after he collapsed on a New York sidewalk. [This statement is a *fact;* it can be proved.]

2. From the article, you can predict that if the public had continued to support Shipwreck Kelly,

☐ a. he would have quit while his popularity was still high.

☒ b. he would have continued to perform crazy stunts.

☐ c. he would have trained his son to follow in his footsteps.

3. Choose from the letters below to correctly complete the following statement. Write the letters on the lines.

On the positive side, ____*c*____, but on the negative side ____*a*____.

a. Kelly risked his life needlessly

b. Kelly survived five shipwrecks, two airplane crashes, three automobile accidents, and a train wreck

c. Kelly entertained thousands of people during the 1920s

4. What was the cause of the difficulty Kelly had walking after sitting on the flagpole in Atlantic City?

☐ a. It took him four minutes to descend the pole.

☐ b. Twenty thousand screaming fans greeted him when he hit the ground.

☒ c. He hadn't taken a step in over 49 days, and so his legs were weak.

5. What did you have to do to answer question 4?

☐ a. find an opinion (what someone thinks about something)

☒ b. find a cause (why something happened)

☐ c. find a comparison (how things are the same)

____5____ Number of correct answers

Record your personal assessment of your work on the Critical Thinking Chart on page 74.

Personal Response

How do you think Shipwreck Kelly felt when the public lost interest in him?

[Use your own experience and facts from the article to draw a

conclusion.]

_____

_____

Self-Assessment

What concepts or ideas from the article were difficult to understand?

[Try to recall anything in the article that gave you trouble.]

_____

_____

Which were easy to understand?

[Record the parts of the article that you understood with no

difficulty.]

_____

Self-Assessment

To get the most out of the Critical Reading series program, you need to take charge of your own progress in improving your reading comprehension and critical thinking skills. Here are some of the features that help you work on those essential skills.

Reading Comprehension Exercises. Complete these exercises immediately after reading the article. They help you recall what you have read, understand the stated and implied main ideas, and add words to your working vocabulary.

Critical Thinking Skills Exercises. These exercises help you focus on the author's approach and purpose, recognize and generate summaries and paraphrases, and identify relationships between ideas.

Personal Response and Self-assessment. Questions in this category help you relate the articles to your personal experience and give you the opportunity to evaluate your understanding of the information in that lesson.

Compare and Contrast Charts. At the end of each unit you will complete a Compare and Contrast chart. The completed chart helps you see what the articles have in common and gives you an opportunity to explore your own ideas about the topics discussed in the articles.

The Graphs. The graphs and charts at the end of each unit enable you to keep track of your progress. Check your graphs regularly with your teacher. Decide whether your progress is satisfactory or whether you need additional work on some skills. What types of exercises are you having difficulty with? Talk with your teacher about ways to work on the skills in which you need the most practice.

UNIT ONE

SNOWFLAKE BENTLEY
A Fascination with Snow

The winter wind swept through the tiny village of Jericho, Vermont. Then the first snow of the 1880–1881 season began to fall. Most people took that as a good enough reason to stay inside. But Wilson "Willie Bentley" had other ideas. He pulled on his boots. Then he grabbed his coat, cap, and mittens and headed for the door.

2   Willie loved everything about the outdoors, but he especially loved the snow. Of course, other 15-year-olds loved snow too. But Willie's love went beyond sledding and snowball fights. He wanted to actually study the white stuff. So into the driving storm Willie trudged, carrying the new microscope his mother had given him. He caught a few snowflakes and placed them gently under his microscope. Looking down at them magnified thousands of times, Willie gasped. The snowflakes were all so beautiful, and they were all different. Their unique qualities, however, were lost forever when the snowflakes melted. Somehow, Willie thought, he had to capture their beauty.

3   At first Willie thought he could sketch each snowflake. So he set up a workshop

Snowflakes photographed by Wilson Bentley. Bentley used a special camera to capture these images.

in an unheated woodshed. He borrowed a piece of black velvet from his mother and used the swatch of fabric to catch snowflakes. After gathering a few prize samples, he would dash back to the woodshed and place the snowflakes under his microscope. Then Willie would sketch as fast as he could. But he was never quite fast enough. The snowflake always melted before he could draw an accurate picture.

4   Willie's odd behavior caught everyone's attention. His father felt that Willie was wasting his time. Charlie, Willie's older brother, thought he was nuts. Most of the neighbors in Jericho shared that opinion. Still, Willie would not give up. He hoped that someday people would understand the beauty he saw in snowflakes. But for the moment his most urgent concern was finding a better way to preserve that beauty.

5   He spent hours striving to improve his sketches. Then one day he had a bright idea. He saw an advertisement for a special camera that could be attached to a microscope. With a camera like that, Willie thought, he could photograph snowflakes. He would then be able to keep a permanent record of each spectacular snowflake. Unfortunately, the camera cost a hundred dollars. In the 1880s, that was a lot of money to a poor farmer like Willie's

father. Besides, what would the neighbors say? A man would have to be crazy to spend a hundred dollars so that his son could take pictures of snow.

6   Mr. Bentley wasn't crazy, and he still couldn't make sense of his son's hobby, but he loved to see Willie happy. So he

and his wife cut some corners to save money. Month after month they put aside a few dollars. On Willie's 17th birthday, Mr. and Mrs. Bentley presented their son with the special camera.

7   No one had ever photographed snowflakes before, so there were no books

Wilson Bentley photographing snowflakes with his special camera

or manuals explaining how to go about it. Willie had to resort to trial and error. He tried one method after another. On January 15, 1885, he finally got it right. He took a perfect photograph of a snowflake.

8   Willie, who had come to be nicknamed Snowflake, wanted to do nothing but photograph snowflakes. And for the next 46 years that is exactly what he did. He never married. He never moved from the farmhouse where he was born. Snowflake Bentley managed to survive by doing some farming and writing magazine articles. The money he made from the sale of his photos he spent on new equipment.

9   Willie lived for the next snowstorm. Townspeople got used to seeing him outdoors at the strangest hours and in the foulest weather. If it began snowing during mealtime, he would stop eating and dash outside. If a storm lasted all night, Willie would forget about sleeping. It seemed that he was always chasing one snowflake or another. He couldn't bear the thought that some great snowflake might escape his lens.

10   By 1931 Willie had photographed 5,381 snowflakes. People all over the world knew of his work. His book, *Snow Crystals*, was published in November 1931. Still, for Willie, now 66 years old, a new winter meant new snowflakes. In early December, he gave a lecture in a neighboring town. That night a terrible blizzard struck. Friends strongly urged Willie to stay in town. But Willie would have none of it. He loved wild snowstorms; they often yielded the best photos. So he wrapped a scarf around his neck and walked the six miles back to his house. When he finally staggered into his farmhouse, he was shaking all over.

11   The next day Willie fell ill. At first he insisted that he would get better. But he didn't. He only got worse. Finally Willie's nephew, who shared the farmhouse with him, called in the doctor. But it was too late. Snowflake Bentley died two days before Christmas. 🍂

If you have been timed while reading this article, enter your reading time below. Then turn to the Words-per-Minute Table on page 71 and look up your reading speed (words per minute). Enter your reading speed on the graph on page 72.

Reading Time: Lesson 1

_____ : _____
Minutes   Seconds

A | Finding the Main Idea

One statement below expresses the main idea of the article. One statement is too general, or too broad. The other statement explains only part of the article; it is too narrow. Label the statements using the following key:

M—Main Idea　　　**B—Too Broad**　　　**N—Too Narrow**

_____ 1. Wilson Snowflake Bentley, who lived his whole life in Jericho, Vermont, loved snow.

_____ 2. Snowflake Bentley put together a book about snowflakes.

_____ 3 Wilson Snowflake Bentley devoted his life to capturing snowflakes on film.

_____ Score 15 points for a correct M answer.

_____ Score 5 points for each correct B or N answer.

_____ **Total Score:** Finding the Main Idea

B | Recalling Facts

How well do you remember the facts in the article? Put an X in the box next to the answer that correctly completes each statement about the article.

1. Willie set up his workshop in
   - ☐ a. the kitchen of his family's farmhouse.
   - ☐ b. an unheated woodshed.
   - ☐ c. a friend's house.

2. Wilson Bentley was the first person ever to
   - ☐ a. photograph snowflakes.
   - ☐ b. catch snowflakes.
   - ☐ c. walk six miles in a snowstorm.

3. Willie caught his snowflakes
   - ☐ a. in his hand.
   - ☐ b. on a cold piece of glass.
   - ☐ c. on a piece of black velvet.

4. Before getting his camera, Willie tried to preserve the beauty of snowflakes by
   - ☐ a. storing them on ice.
   - ☐ b. writing articles about them.
   - ☐ c. sketching them.

5. Willie never slept
   - ☐ a. when it was dark outside.
   - ☐ b. during a snowstorm.
   - ☐ c. more than four hours a night.

Score 5 points for each correct answer.

_____ **Total Score:** Recalling Facts

C | Making Inferences

When you combine your own experience and information from a text to draw a conclusion that is not directly stated in that text, you are making an inference. Below are five statements that may or may not be inferences based on information in the article. Label the statements using the following key:

C—Correct Inference   F—Faulty Inference

_____ 1. Almost everyone in Jericho, Vermont, knew Snowflake Bentley.

_____ 2. Willie liked winters more than he liked summers.

_____ 3. When photographing snowflakes, Willie often worked with partners.

_____ 4. Snowflake Bentley was a lonely man.

_____ 5. Snowflake Bentley died in poverty.

Score 5 points for each correct answer.

_____ **Total Score:** Making Inferences

D | Using Words Precisely

Each numbered sentence below contains an underlined word or phrase from the article. Following the sentence are three definitions. One definition is closest to the meaning of the underlined word. One definition is opposite or nearly opposite. Label those two definitions using the following key. Do not label the remaining definition.

C—Closest   O—Opposite or Nearly Opposite

1. The snowflakes always melted before he could draw an <u>accurate</u> picture.

_____ a. correct

_____ b. inexact

_____ c. pretty

2. He spent hours <u>striving</u> to improve his sketches.

_____ a. trying

_____ b. drawing

_____ c. quitting

3. Willie had to <u>resort to</u> trial and error.

_____ a. learn about

_____ b. use

_____ c. give up on

4. Townspeople got used to seeing him outdoors at the strangest hours and in the <u>foulest</u> weather.

_____ a. nicest

_____ b. oddest

_____ c. nastiest

5. He loved wild snowstorms: they often <u>yielded</u> the best photos.

_____ a. observed

_____ b. provided

_____ c. withheld

_____ Score 3 points for each correct C answer.

_____ Score 2 points for each correct O answer.

_____ **Total Score:** Using Words Precisely

Enter the four total scores in the spaces below, and add them together to find your Reading Comprehension Score. Then record your score on the graph on page 73.

Score	Question Type	Lesson 1
_____	Finding the Main Idea	
_____	Recalling Facts	
_____	Making Inferences	
_____	Using Words Precisely	
_____	**Reading Comprehension Score**	

Author's Approach

Put an X in the box next to the correct answer.

1. The main purpose of the first paragraph is to

☐ a. reveal that Willie loved to be out in the snow.

☐ b. describe winter in Vermont.

☐ c. express an opinion about Willie's odd behavior.

2. From the statements below, choose those that you believe the author would agree with.

☐ a. Willie lived the way he wanted to live.

☐ b. Willie died a sad, crazy old man.

☐ c. Willie saw beauty in things that most other people ignore.

3. Judging by the statement from the article "Townspeople got used to seeing him outdoors at the strangest hours and in the foulest weather," you can conclude that the author wants the reader to think that

☐ a. Willie's neighbors respected Willie's devotion to his hobby.

☐ b. Willie's neighbors eventually came to accept his fascination with snow.

☐ c. Willie's neighbors tried to prevent him from going outside in bad weather.

4. In this article, "So he and his wife cut some corners to save money" means

☐ a. Willie's parents asked their neighbors to lend them some money.

☐ b. Willie's parents clipped coupons in order to save money.

☐ c. Willie's parents made some sacrifices in order to save money.

_____ Number of correct answers

Record your personal assessment of your work on the Critical Thinking Chart on page 74.

CRITICAL THINKING

Summarizing and Paraphrasing

Follow the directions provided for question 1. Put an X in the box next to the correct answer for the other questions.

1. Look for the important ideas and events in paragraphs 2 and 3. Summarize those paragraphs in one or two sentences.

_____

_____

_____

_____

2. Below are summaries of the article. Choose the summary that says all the most important things about the article but in the fewest words.

☐ a. After his parents gave him a special camera, Willie Bentley was able to take perfect photographs of snowflakes. He spent the rest of his life chasing individual flakes and capturing their beauty on film.

☐ b. Willie Bentley became so fascinated by snowflakes that he spent his life photographing their beauty.

☐ c. Willie Bentley lived to run out into the snow and capture individual snowflakes.

CRITICAL THINKING

3. Choose the sentence that correctly restates the following sentence from the article:

"Mr. Bentley wasn't crazy, and he still couldn't make sense of his son's hobby, but he loved to see Willie happy."

☐ a. Mr. Bentley thought that his son was crazy.

☐ b. Mr. Bentley couldn't figure out why photographing snowflakes made his son so happy.

☐ c. Even though Mr. Bentley didn't understand Willie's hobby, he supported his son because photographing snowflakes made Willie happy.

_____ Number of correct answers

Record your personal assessment of your work on the Critical Thinking Chart on page 74.

Critical Thinking

Put an X in the box next to the correct answer for questions 1 and 3. Follow the directions provided for the other questions.

1. From Willie Bentley's actions as described in this article, you can predict that if you asked him about his final walk home in the blizzard, he would say that

☐ a. he was frightened all the way home.

☐ b. he regretted walking home in the blizzard.

☐ c. he enjoyed taking photographs of snowflakes along the way.

2. Choose from the letters below to correctly complete the following statement. Write the letters on the lines.

In the article, _____ and _____ are different.

a. Willie's reaction to a snowstorm

b. his neighbors' reaction to a snowstorm

c. his parents' reaction to a snowstorm

3. What was the effect of Willie's six-mile walk home through a blizzard in December 1931?

☐ a. He became ill and died.

☐ b. He published a book of his photographs called *Snow Crystals*.

☐ c. Friends urged him to stay in town.

4. Which paragraphs from the article provide evidence that supports your answer to question 3?

_____

_____ Number of correct answers

Record your personal assessment of your work on the Critical Thinking Chart on page 74.

Personal Response

1. Why do you think Willie Bentley photographed snowflakes?

_____

_____

_____

2. Just before he died, Willie Bentley walked home through a terrible blizzard. Describe a time when you were out in a powerful storm similar to that one.

_____

_____

_____

_____

Self-Assessment

I was confused on question # _____ in section _____ because

_____

_____

_____

_____

BLACK BART
Gentle Bandit

The Wells Fargo & Company Express Office on C Street in Virginia City, Nevada, around 1866. The stage coach parked in front is of the type that Black Bart robbed.

Charley Bolton was fed up. All his life he had struggled just to eke out a living. Though he loved his wife, Mary, and his three small daughters, he was tired of living in poverty. At the age of 45, he longed to start a new life. He wanted travel, excitement, and riches. So in 1875 Charley abandoned his family in Illinois and moved to California. He gave up his old values of honesty and hard work. He became Black Bart, the stagecoach robber. (Black Bart was a tough-sounding name he adopted for himself.)

2   Over the next eight years, Black Bart committed a total of 28 robberies against the Wells Fargo Company. Not one of those robberies made him rich. By the 1870s, the California Gold Rush had ended. Wells Fargo stagecoaches no longer carried huge sums of cash. But although the holdups did not make Bart rich, they certainly did make him famous. By the time of his arrest in 1883, Black Bart was known throughout northern California.

3   Bart won his fame by capturing the imagination of the people. He approached

crime in such an offbeat way that folks couldn't help but like him. For one thing, while most bandits worked with partners, Bart always worked alone. Although he carried a gun, he never fired a shot. He never even roughed anyone up. And while all other roadside bandits used horses to make their getaways, Bart worked on foot. After each holdup, he simply walked off into the woods. That led to many exaggerated stories about him. Some people claimed that he was a wild man who appeared out of nowhere and vanished into thin air. Some viewed him as an agent of the devil. Some even believed he was a ghost.

4   One other thing set Black Bart apart from all the other robbers of his era: his manners. During his holdups, Bart spoke politely. He waited patiently to collect the loot. Then he calmly told the stagecoach driver to go on with his route.

5   The robbery Bart committed on July 25, 1878, showed his special flair. For months he studied the stagecoach route, which ran through the mountains of north central California. After much thought, he picked a spot for the holdup. It was a deserted place near a sharp bend in the road. Bart got to the spot bright and early. Dressed in a business suit and derby, he looked quite dapper.

6   Soon, though, he reached into his bag and pulled out a flour sack and a bathrobe. He slipped the bathrobe on over his suit. The flour sack, which had two eyeholes cut in it, he pulled over his hat and face. Clad in that ridiculous costume, Bart waited in the bushes until he heard the stage coming. Then he jumped into the middle of the road and pointed his rifle at the driver. Frightened, the driver brought the horses to a halt. "Throw down the box," Bart said softly.

7   The Wells Fargo box contained all the money and mail to be delivered that day. The driver did as Bart asked. When Bart had the box in his hand, he spoke to the driver again. "All right," he said, "you may drive on."

8   As the stagecoach thundered out of sight, Bart gave a friendly wave to the startled driver. Then he pulled an ax from his bag and chopped open the Wells Fargo box. Inside he found 600 dollars. Bart scooped up the money and put it in his bag. Next he took off the bathrobe and flour sack and stuffed those in the bag too. Finally, Bart grabbed a piece of mail from the Wells Fargo box and took out a pencil. Impulsively, he wrote a short poem on the back of the envelope. It read:

Yet come what will, I'll try it once
My condition can't be worse;
And if there's money in that box
Tis money in my purse.
He signed it "Black Bart, the Po 8."

Portrait of Black Bart, Gentleman Bandit

9   With a smile on his face, Bart put the poem back in the box. It would be his gift to the detectives who tried to track him down. Then Bart picked up his bags and headed off through the mountains. He walked for several hours before reaching a small town. In the town he introduced himself as a traveling businessman. He then caught a ride to a distant city, far from the scene of the crime.

10   As word of the robberies spread, Bart became more and more popular. The soft voice, the silly disguise, and the poems made him a hot topic of conversation. Black Bart continued his life of well-mannered crime until November 3, 1883, when he finally met up with a piece of bad luck. He held up a stagecoach bound for Milton, California. By that time the Wells Fargo Company had started bolting its boxes to the floors of stagecoaches in hopes of discouraging bandits like Black Bart. It didn't work. Bart simply climbed into the stagecoach and chopped the box open. Before he got started, he ordered the driver to unhitch the horses and take them down the road. He told the driver to wait there until he'd finished the robbery.

11   As luck would have it, on this particular day a young boy was hunting in the nearby woods. Seeing the driver and horses waiting around in the road, the boy realized what was happening. Quietly he joined the driver, and the two of them crept back to the stagecoach. By the time they reached it, Bart had collected the money and was heading into the woods. The boy quickly took aim with his

hunting rifle and fired. The bullet nicked Bart, causing him to drop the money bag.

12   Bart managed to escape into the woods, but the damage had been done. When the Wells Fargo detective examined the contents of the bag, he found a handkerchief. The handkerchief had a laundry mark. Using that clue, the detective tracked down the owner. A week later, in San Francisco, the police arrested the infamous Black Bart.

13   At first Bart denied everything. Under persistent questioning, though, he finally confessed. When he'd told his story to the police, newspaper reporters across the state wrote articles glorifying him. Still, the court found Bart guilty and sentenced him to six years at San Quentin Prison. Before being led away, however, Black Bart told the judge one last thing. He had never wanted to hurt anyone. It was true he had held a rifle, but it had never been loaded. 🍃

If you have been timed while reading this article, enter your reading time below. Then turn to the Words-per-Minute Table on page 71 and look up your reading speed (words per minute). Enter your reading speed on the graph on page 72.

Reading Time: Lesson 2

_____ : _____
Minutes   *Seconds*

A Finding the Main Idea

One statement below expresses the main idea of the article. One statement is too general, or too broad. The other statement explains only part of the article; it is too narrow. Label the statements using the following key:

M—Main Idea   **B—Too Broad**   **N—Too Narrow**

_____ 1. Black Bart left his home and family to become a stagecoach robber.

_____ 2. Black Bart became famous as a polite, colorful, and nonviolent stagecoach robber.

_____ 3. Black Bart was a famous robber in the late 1800s.

_____ Score 15 points for a correct M answer.

_____ Score 5 points for each correct B or N answer.

_____ **Total Score:** Finding the Main Idea

B Recalling Facts

How well do you remember the facts in the article? Put an X in the box next to the answer that correctly completes each statement about the article.

1. When Black Bart committed a robbery, he always worked
    ☐ a. with two partners.
    ☐ b. alone.
    ☐ c. on horseback.

2. Black Bart left a poem
    ☐ a. on the driver's seat of a stagecoach.
    ☐ b. in the saddlebag of a horse.
    ☐ c. in a Wells Fargo box.

3. Bart committed his robberies wearing
    ☐ a. women's clothing.
    ☐ b. a bathrobe.
    ☐ c. a clown suit.

4. The clue that finally led to the capture of Black Bart was a
    ☐ a. laundry mark on a handkerchief.
    ☐ b. poem that Black Bart left on an envelope.
    ☐ c. bullet that matched the gun Black Bart used.

5. After his trial, Black Bart was
    ☐ a. released.
    ☐ b. sentenced to six years in prison.
    ☐ c. sent back to Illinois.

Score 5 points for each correct answer.

_____ **Total Score:** Recalling Facts

C | Making Inferences

When you combine your own experience and information from a text to draw a conclusion that is not directly stated in that text, you are making an inference. Below are five statements that may or may not be inferences based on information in the article. Label the statements using the following key:

C—Correct Inference   **F—Faulty Inference**

_____ 1. During the California Gold Rush, Wells Fargo stagecoaches carried huge sums of cash.

_____ 2. To Black Bart, adventure was more important than family.

_____ 3. Black Bart was one of the most feared robbers of his day.

_____ 4. Black Bart lived by himself in the woods.

_____ 5. Black Bart enjoyed his life as a stage coach robber.

Score 5 points for each correct answer.

_____ **Total Score:** Making Inferences

D | Using Words Precisely

Each numbered sentence below contains an underlined word or phrase from the article. Following the sentence are three definitions. One definition is closest to the meaning of the underlined word. One definition is opposite or nearly opposite. Label those two definitions using the following key. Do not label the remaining definition.

C—Closest   **O—Opposite or Nearly Opposite**

1. Dressed in a business suit and derby, he looked quite <u>dapper</u>.

_____ a. dowdy

_____ b. stylish

_____ c. ridiculous

2. <u>Impulsively</u>, he wrote a short poem on the back of the envelope.

_____ a. on the spur of the moment

_____ b. after much planning

_____ c. while standing up

3. A week later, in San Francisco, the police arrested the <u>infamous</u> Black Bart.

_____ a. well respected

_____ b. having a bad reputation

_____ c. handsome

4. Under <u>persistent</u> questioning, though, he finally confessed.

_____ a. likely to stop for almost any reason

_____ b. confused

_____ c. repeated and continuing

5. When he'd told his story to the police, newspaper reporters across the state wrote articles <u>glorifying</u> him.

_____ a. praising

_____ b. questioning

_____ c. condemning

_____ Score 3 points for each correct C answer.

_____ Score 2 points for each correct O answer.

_____ **Total Score:** Using Words Precisely

Enter the four total scores in the spaces below, and add them together to find your Reading Comprehension Score. Then record your score on the graph on page 73.

Score	Question Type	Lesson 2
_____	Finding the Main Idea	
_____	Recalling Facts	
_____	Making Inferences	
_____	Using Words Precisely	
_____	**Reading Comprehension Score**	

Author's Approach

Put an X in the box next to the correct answer.

1. What does the author mean by the statement "As word of the robberies spread, Bart became more and more popular"?

☐ a. After people learned about Bart's robberies, they wanted him to be arrested.

☐ b. After other robbers learned about Bart, they began imitating his style.

☐ c. As people heard about the polite way Bart committed his robberies, they started to like him.

2. Choose the statement below that is the weakest argument for claiming that Bart should not have gone to jail.

☐ a. Bart stole hundreds of dollars from the Wells Fargo Company.

☐ b. The rifle he used during holdups was not loaded.

☐ c. Bart was always friendly and polite during his robberies.

3. How is the author's purpose for writing the article expressed in paragraph 6?

☐ a. The author explains how stagecoach robbers prepared themselves before committing a crime.

☐ b. The author paints an amusing picture by describing Bart's disguise.

☐ c. The author conveys a mood of fear before the stagecoach robbery takes place.

CRITICAL THINKING

4. The author probably wrote this article in order to

☐ a. entertain the reader with a story about a gentleman bandit.

☐ b. inform the reader about crime in the late 1800s.

☐ c. compare Black Bart's techniques to those of other bandits.

_____ Number of correct answers

Record your personal assessment of your work on the Critical Thinking Chart on page 74.

Summarizing and Paraphrasing

Put an X in the box next to the correct answer.

1. Below are summaries of the article. Choose the summary that says all the most important things about the article but in the fewest words.

☐ a. Black Bart held up Wells Fargo stagecoaches in the late 1870s and early 1880s. During the holdups, he spoke politely and even left a poem behind as a clue for the detectives. After he was arrested and sentenced to six years at San Quentin Prison, Bart told the judge that he had never used a loaded rifle during the holdups.

☐ b. Black Bart robbed stagecoaches until he was arrested in 1883. After his sentencing, Bart told the judge that he had never used a loaded rifle.

☐ c. A stagecoach robber in the late 1800s, Black Bart became famous for his good manners, silly disguises, and signed poems. After his arrest and sentencing in 1883, Bart admitted that the rifle he had used during the holdups had never been loaded.

2. Choose the best one-sentence paraphrase for the following sentence from the article:

When he'd told his story to the police, newspaper reporters across the state wrote articles glorifying him.

☐ a. While Bart was speaking to the police, newspaper reporters were writing false stories about him.

☐ b. After Bart confessed to the police, newspaper reporters wrote articles that made him seem like a hero.

☐ c. Bart lied to the police and then newspaper reporters printed his story.

_____ Number of correct answers

Record your personal assessment of your work on the Critical Thinking Chart on page 74.

Critical Thinking

Put an X in the box next to the correct answer for questions 1, 3, and 4. Follow the directions provided for the other questions.

1. From the article, you can predict that if a stagecoach driver had pulled a gun on Black Bart,

☐ a. Bart would have politely laid down his rifle.

☐ b. Bart would have shot the driver.

☐ c. Bart would have shouted angrily at the driver.

2. Using what you know about a modern bank robber and what is told about Black Bart in the article, name three ways Black Bart is similar to and different from a modern bank robber. Cite the paragraph number(s) where you found details in the article to support your conclusions.

Similarities

_____

_____

_____

Differences

_____

_____

_____

3. What was the cause of Bart's capture and arrest?

☐ a. The Wells Fargo Company began bolting its boxes to the floors of stagecoaches.

☐ b. Bart confessed his crimes.

☐ c. A detective traced the laundry mark on a handkerchief Bart had left in the money bag.

4. How is Black Bart an example of an eccentric?

☐ a. He does not fit most people's idea of a robber.

☐ b. He abandoned his family in Illinois and moved to California.

☐ c. He robbed stagecoaches in California.

5. In which paragraph did you find your information or details to answer question 3?

_____

_____ Number of correct answers

Record your personal assessment of your work on the Critical Thinking Chart on page 74.

Personal Response

Would you recommend this article to other students? Explain.

_____

_____

_____

_____

Self-Assessment

I'm proud of how I answered question # _____ in section _____ because

_____

_____

_____

_____

CRITICAL THINKING

GEORGE KAUFMAN
Keeping Fit

George Kaufman, at the typewriter, working with collaborator Moss Hart. Kaufman and Hart collaborated on plays that are still popular today, such as The Man Who Came to Dinner.

George Kaufman hated doorknobs. To be more accurate, he feared doorknobs. He feared the dirt that built up on them. He feared the fingerprints that people left on them. Above all, he feared the diseases he believed he could catch from them. As a young man, Kaufman became convinced that all doorknobs were dirty. As he saw it, an average doorknob collected germs from dozens of unclean hands every day. So he went through life avoiding contact with the filthy things. He never put his bare hand on a doorknob. When he needed to open a door, we would stick his hand into his jacket pocket and, with the fabric protecting him, grab the doorknob.

2   Luckily, his fear did not interfere with his work. From 1920 until his death in 1961, Kaufman wrote more than 40 Broadway plays. They included such smash hits as *Dinner at Eight, You Can't Take It with You,* and *The Man Who Came to Dinner.* Despite his success, though, Kaufman remained a man plagued by fears. His fear of doorknobs was not an isolated quirk. He also dreaded dust,

horses, cheese, roast goose, foreign countries, and many other things. He despised everything that struck him as unclean. He hated shaking hands. He could picture thousands of tiny germs jumping from the other person's hand onto his. He loathed eating in restaurants because he could never be sure the silverware had been sterilized. He disliked eating at friends' houses for the same reason.

3   Kaufman's fears all stemmed from the same source. He was uncommonly worried about his health. Kaufman had no real health problems until he was in his late fifties. But that didn't matter. The point was that he believed he had problems. His fears caused him real anguish. Sometimes he focused on his teeth. It seemed to him that they were about to fall out. To reassure himself, he saw his dentist at least six times a year. He also became preoccupied with his eyes. He was sure he was going blind. To avoid eyestrain, he bought several different pairs of glasses. Whenever he needed to refocus his vision, he would change glasses.

4   Because Kaufman was rich, famous, and successful, many people did not realize the depth of his fears. But every day, day after day, he tortured himself with his thoughts. He would not go near

open windows, fearing that a sudden chill would injure his lungs. He always took his own breakfast cereal with him when traveling. He feared that the chefs of even the best hotels might contaminate the food.

5   To Kaufman, the world seemed fraught with danger. He had nightmares in which he developed ulcers, heart trouble, cancer. If a friend had a bad cough, he assumed that he would catch it. In fact, he would begin preparing for a serious lung disease. If someone had a headache, Kaufman's head would begin to throb. Within hours he would have himself convinced that he had a brain tumor.

6   Kaufman sometimes tried to hide his worries by making jokes. He once made a humorous remark about a man who was a year older than he. "I watch him very carefully," Kaufman said, "to see what I'm going to catch next year." Most people laughed at that line, not guessing that it contained a great deal of truth.

7   In an effort to protect his health, Kaufman put himself in the care of all kinds of medical specialists. He had doctors looking out for his feet, his back, and his internal organs. He hired one doctor to tend to his nervous system. He hired another to keep tabs on his circulation. He hired a third to provide

psychiatric counseling. He even hired a specialist to give him treatments to prevent baldness.

8   Kaufman felt he could not survive without his doctors. But that did not mean he treated them well. He was often

Copy of the 1939 Playbill *for* The Man Who Came to Dinner

demanding and unreasonable with them. He resented any personal questions they asked. He refused to accept their diagnoses that he was healthy. He insisted that they give him injections even though he wasn't sick. As long as he was getting a shot, he felt he was being helped.

9   Once, late on a Sunday night, Kaufman called Dr. Menard Gertler. Gertler had just become Kaufman's personal physician. "I need you immediately," Kaufman said when Gertler answered the phone. Then Kaufman hung up. Gertler grabbed his medical bag and rushed out the door. Arriving at Kaufman's apartment building, he announced that there was a medical emergency in Kaufman's apartment. He asked the elevator operator to take him up directly. When Gertler burst into Kaufman's room, however, he found his patient standing in the middle of the floor, holding a stopwatch in his hand. Shocked, Gertler asked for an explanation. Said Kaufman calmly, "I wanted to see how long it would take you to get here if I were *really* ill." 🍂

If you have been timed while reading this article, enter your reading time below. Then turn to the Words-per-Minute Table on page 71 and look up your reading speed (words per minute). Enter your reading speed on the graph on page 72.

Reading Time: **Lesson 3**

_____ : _____
Minutes   Seconds

A Finding the Main Idea

One statement below expresses the main idea of the article. One statement is too general, or too broad. The other statement explains only part of the article; it is too narrow. Label the statements using the following key:

M—Main Idea   **B—Too Broad**   **N—Too Narrow**

_____ 1. George Kaufman was an American playwright who wrote more than 40 Broadway plays.

_____ 2. George Kaufman's life was dominated by a fear of germs and diseases.

_____ 3. George Kaufman lived a life filled with fear.

_____ Score 15 points for a correct M answer.

_____ Score 5 points for each correct B or N answer.

_____ **Total Score:** Finding the Main Idea

B Recalling Facts

How well do you remember the facts in the article? Put an X in the box next to the answer that correctly completes each statement about the article.

1. Kaufman always kept his hand in his jacket pocket when
   - ☐ a. shaking hands.
   - ☐ b. opening doors.
   - ☐ c. eating.

2. Kaufman feared he
   - ☐ a. had no true friends.
   - ☐ b. was going blind.
   - ☐ c. would lose the ability to write good plays.

3. When traveling, Kaufman always brought along his own
   - ☐ a. breakfast cereal.
   - ☐ b. silverware.
   - ☐ c. medical books.

4. Kaufman had nightmares in which
   - ☐ a. he was chased by giant doorknobs.
   - ☐ b. his teeth fell out.
   - ☐ c. he developed cancer.

5. Kaufman did not like his doctors to
   - ☐ a. give him shots.
   - ☐ b. tell him bad news.
   - ☐ c. ask him personal questions.

Score 5 points for each correct answer.

_____ **Total Score:** Recalling Facts

C | Making Inferences

When you combine your own experience and information from a text to draw a conclusion that is not directly stated in that text, you are making an inference. Below are five statements that may or may not be inferences based on information in the article. Label the statements using the following key:

C—Correct Inference   **F—Faulty Inference**

_____ 1. Kaufman thought that most doctors were quacks.

_____ 2. Kaufman had many friends who were seriously ill.

_____ 3. Kaufman felt that horses were unclean.

_____ 4. After Kaufman called him for nothing, Dr. Gertler resigned as his personal physician.

_____ 5. Kaufman lived in the city.

Score 5 points for each correct answer.

_____ **Total Score:** Making Inferences

D | Using Words Precisely

Each numbered sentence below contains an underlined word or phrase from the article. Following the sentence are three definitions. One definition is closest to the meaning of the underlined word. One definition is opposite or nearly opposite. Label those two definitions using the following key. Do not label the remaining definition.

C—Closest   **O—Opposite or Nearly Opposite**

1. His fear of doorknobs was not an isolated <u>quirk</u>.

_____ a. peculiarity

_____ b. common trait

_____ c. terror

2. He <u>loathed</u> eating in restaurants because he could never be sure the silverware had been sterilized.

_____ a. loved

_____ b. avoided

_____ c. hated

3. His fears caused him real <u>anguish</u>.

_____ a. admiration

_____ b. distress

_____ c. joy

4. He feared that the chefs of even the best hotels might <u>contaminate</u> the food.

_____ a. purify

_____ b. pollute

_____ c. taste

5. To Kaufman, the world seemed <u>fraught with</u> danger.

_____ a. filled with

_____ b. lacking

_____ c. comfortable with

_____ Score 3 points for each correct C answer.

_____ Score 2 points for each correct O answer.

_____ **Total Score:** Using Words Precisely

Enter the four total scores in the spaces below, and add them together to find your Reading Comprehension Score. Then record your score on the graph on page 73.

Score	Question Type	Lesson 3
_____	Finding the Main Idea	
_____	Recalling Facts	
_____	Making Inferences	
_____	Using Words Precisely	
_____	**Reading Comprehension Score**	

Author's Approach

Put an X in the box next to the correct answer.

1. The main purpose of the first paragraph is to
   - ☐ a. inform the reader about the uncleanliness of doorknobs.
   - ☐ b. express an opinion about the uncleanliness of doorknobs.
   - ☐ c. introduce Kaufman's obsession with cleanliness.

2. Judging by the statement from the article "To Kaufman, the world seemed fraught with danger," you can conclude that the author wants the reader to think that
   - ☐ a. Kaufman never stopped worrying about his health.
   - ☐ b. Kaufman thought that other people wanted to harm him.
   - ☐ c. Kaufman had an unnatural fear of accidents.

3. The author tells this story mainly by
   - ☐ a. retelling the doctors experiences with Kaufman.
   - ☐ b. comparing Kaufman's fears to those of other writers.
   - ☐ c. telling different stories about Kaufman's concern with his health.

_____ Number of correct answers

Record your personal assessment of your work on the Critical Thinking Chart on page 74.

Summarizing and Paraphrasing

Follow the directions provided for questions 1 and 2. Put an X in the box next to the correct answer for question 3.

1. Complete the following one-sentence summary of the article using the lettered phrases from the phrase bank below. Write the letters on the lines.

> **Phrase Bank:**
> a. his worries about different health problems
> b. his relationship with his doctors
> c. his fear of germs

The article about George Kaufman begins with _____, goes on to explain _____, and ends with _____.

2. Reread paragraph 9 in the article. Below, write a summary of the paragraph in no more than 25 words.

_____

_____

_____

_____

Reread your summary and decide whether it covers important ideas in the paragraph. Next, decide how to shorten the summary to 15 words or less without leaving out any essential information. Write this summary below.

_____

_____

_____

3. Choose the sentence that correctly restates the following sentence from the article:

"When he needed to open a door, he would stick his hand into his jacket pocket and, with the fabric protecting him, grab the doorknob."

☐ a. Kaufman would stick his hand in his pocket and refuse to touch a doorknob.

☐ b. Kaufman opened a door by putting his hand in his pocket and then, protected by the cloth, reaching for the doorknob.

☐ c. Before opening a door, Kaufman cleaned the doorknob with the lining of his jacket pocket.

> _____ Number of correct answers
>
> Record your personal assessment of your work on the Critical Thinking Chart on page 74.

Critical Thinking

Follow the directions provided for questions 1, 3, and 4. Put an X in the box next to the correct answer for the other questions.

1. For each statement below, write O if it expresses an opinion and write F if it expresses a fact.

_____ a. Kaufman put himself in the care of several medical specialists.

_____ b. Kaufman wrote many successful plays in spite of his fears.

_____ c. Kaufman wrote the best plays produced on Broadway in the 1920s and 1930s.

2. Judging by George Kaufman's actions as described in this article, you can predict that

☐ a. he would have been very brave if he were really sick.

☐ b. he would have been easy to live with.

☐ c. he would have been a very difficult patient.

3. Choose from the letters below to correctly complete the following statement. Write the letters on the lines.

On the positive side, _____, but on the negative side _____.

a. Kaufman worried obsessively about his health

b. Kaufman hated shaking hands

c. Kaufman was a successful writer

4. Read paragraph 4. Then choose from the letters below to correctly complete the following statement. Write the letters on the lines.

According to paragraph 4, _____ because _____.

a. Kaufman feared that restaurant chefs would contaminate his food

b. Kaufman always carried his own breakfast cereal

c. Kaufman would not go near open windows

5. What did you have to do to answer question 2?

☐ a. draw a conclusion (a sensible statement based on the text and your experience)

☐ b. find an opinion (what someone thinks about something)

☐ c. find a cause (why something happened)

_____ Number of correct answers

Record your personal assessment of your work on the Critical Thinking Chart on page 74.

Personal Response

1. If I were the author, I would add

_____

_____

because

_____

_____

2. Describe a time when you were afraid of something without a good reason.

_____

_____

_____

Self-Assessment

The part I found most difficult about the article was

_____

_____

I found this difficult because

_____

_____

DORIS DUKE
Poor Little Rich Girl

Doris Duke had everything money could buy. She owned five homes, including a penthouse in New York City and a mansion in Hawaii. She owned hundreds of jewels and tons of gold. She drank thousand-dollar bottles of wine. She traveled in her own $25-million jet. In the end, though, Duke's life illustrated an old cliché: Money can't buy happiness.

2   Duke was born in 1912. Her father was millionaire James Duke. He was founder of the American Tobacco Company. He was also the namesake of Duke University. As a baby, Doris was carried around on a silk pillow. Later she was wrapped in mink and driven about in a Rolls-Royce. Her father, who loved her dearly, tried to protect her from all harm. He thought he was doing her a favor when he taught her to be suspicious of others. James Duke feared people would attach themselves to Doris just to get at her money. So again and again he told her to be wary. His deathbed instructions to her were simple: "Trust no one."

3   Doris took her father's advice. She decided that she would handle her

Tobacco heiress and richest woman in the world Doris Duke at Bailey's Beach in Newport, Rhode Island, 1934

business affairs herself. At age 14, one year after her father died, she sued her mother to gain control of some of her inheritance. By the time she was 21, she had millions at her disposal. She handled her money so well that by the time she died, she was worth well over one billion dollars.

4   When it came to her personal life, however, Duke was not so successful. Her father's words kept ringing in her ears. She said, "After I've gone out with a man a few times, he starts to tell me he loves me. But how can I ever be sure?"

5   At age 22, Duke took a chance by marrying James Cromwell, a man 16 years her senior. The marriage lasted nine years. During much of that time, Duke was miserable. In 1940, she gave birth to her only child—a girl, Arden—who lived less than 24 hours. Duke never quite recovered from the loss. Three years later, she divorced Cromwell on the grounds of cruelty. Cromwell asked for a $7 million divorce settlement, thereby confirming Duke's fears that he had only been after her money.

6   Duke had one other failed marriage. It lasted just a year. This time, though, Duke was prepared for failure. On her wedding day, she had the groom sign a prenuptial agreement, which prevented him from ever getting control of her money.

7   After her second divorce, Duke never went near the altar again. Instead, she turned her attention to other things. She gave millions of dollars to worthy causes. She sang, took piano lessons, and studied belly dancing. She attended lavish parties. She flew all around the world, visiting Paris, the Gobi Desert, Bali. Once when she saw an Asian temple she liked, she had it dismantled and sent home. Then she had it rebuilt, piece by piece, on one of her indoor tennis courts. When she came across a rare species of camel, she had two of them shipped home, as well. They lived at her New Jersey estate, making themselves comfortable in her 30-room manor.

8   Underneath all the glitz and glamour, though, something was missing from Duke's life. She wanted to form a deeper connection to people, but her suspicions got in the way. "She thought everybody was after her money," lamented one acquaintance. "I used to tell her, 'You

Aerial view of Doris Duke's estate in Newport, Rhode Island, where Eduardo Tirella was accidentally killed

know, Doris, some people do like you for yourself.'" But Duke could not quite believe that. And so she remained a sad, lonely woman. Her homes were filled not with friends, but with fierce guard dogs. While she did find some creative ways to fill her lonely hours, the loneliness itself didn't go away.

9   For a while, Duke had one close friend—a set designer named Eduardo Tirella. But one October night in 1966, disaster struck. Duke and Tirella were on their way out of Duke's Rhode Island mansion. When they got to the fence that surrounded the property, Tirella got out to open the gate. Somehow, the gears of the car slipped, and Duke felt the car lurch forward. Before she knew what was happening, Duke had run over Tirella and killed him.

10   In the years that followed, Duke tried new ways to fill the emptiness in her life. She supported a group called the Self-Realization Fellowship. She also became a follower of a Kentucky man who called himself Norbu Chen. He claimed to be the reincarnation of the Dalai Lama, Tibet's spiritual leader. Apparently Duke hoped he would help her find inner peace. "She went to Norbu Chen every couple of weeks," said one source. "He would put on his dagger and robe and grab her toes and give her a jolt."

11   None of Duke's efforts worked. Inner peace still eluded her. Eventually, Duke, who was getting old, began to dread death. She underwent plastic surgery to keep her face looking young. She even had a "magnetic rejuvenation" machine put into one of her homes. It was supposed to restore youth by shooting electric currents through her body.

12   When Duke was 75 years old, she made one last attempt to create a family for herself by adopting a 35-year-old woman named Chandi Heffner. Duke and Chandi shared many interests. They both loved animals. They both loved to dance. And they were both interested in the idea of life after death. In fact, for a while Duke believed Chandi was the reincarnation of Arden, her dead baby daughter.

13   The relationship with her new "daughter" eventually turned sour, however. Duke realized that Chandi was not rich, as she had claimed to be. That made Duke question the woman's motives. She decided Chandi, like all the others, was just out to get her money. She even thought Chandi was trying to kill her in order to inherit the Duke fortune. One day Duke told her old dance teacher that Chandi had tried to poison her.

14   In 1988, five years after the adoption, Duke drew up a new will, which cut Chandi out completely. In the will, Duke stated, "I am convinced that I should not have adopted Chandi Heffner. I have come to the realization that her primary motive was financial gain."

15   With Chandi out of the picture, Duke turned to the last contact she had: her butler Bernard Lafferty. In the final months of Duke's life, Lafferty became the closest thing Duke had to a friend. He would talk to her, sit with her, and make sure her meals were prepared exactly as she wished. Of course, he was paid to do all these things. So perhaps in a bizarre way, Doris's father had been right. When Doris Duke died, at age 80, the only ones at her bedside were the butler, a cook, and a maid—all people who were with her because of her money.

If you have been timed while reading this article, enter your reading time below. Then turn to the Words-per-Minute Table on page 71 and look up your reading speed (words per minute). Enter your reading speed on the graph on page 72.

Reading Time: Lesson 4

_____ : _____
Minutes   Seconds

A | Finding the Main Idea

One statement below expresses the main idea of the article. One statement is too general, or too broad. The other statement explains only part of the article; it is too narrow. Label the statements using the following key:

M—Main Idea   B—Too Broad   N—Too Narrow

_____ 1. Five years after adopting Chandi Heffner, Doris Duke cut the woman out of her will completely.

_____ 2. Many rich people are suspicious of those who want to befriend them.

_____ 3. In spite of her great wealth, Doris Duke was unhappy because she questioned the motives of those who tried to become close to her.

_____ Score 15 points for a correct M answer.

_____ Score 5 points for each correct B or N answer.

_____ **Total Score:** Finding the Main Idea

B | Recalling Facts

How well do you remember the facts in the article? Put an X in the box next to the answer that correctly completes each statement about the article.

1. One year after her father died, Doris Duke
   - ☐ a. was worth well over one billion dollars.
   - ☐ b. sued her mother to gain control of some of her inheritance.
   - ☐ c. married James Cromwell.

2. Duke's marriage to James Cromwell lasted
   - ☐ a. just a year.
   - ☐ b. less than 24 hours.
   - ☐ c. nine years.

3. Duke accidentally killed her friend
   - ☐ a. Chandi Heffner.
   - ☐ b. Norbu Chen.
   - ☐ c. Eduardo Tirella.

4. Doris Duke cut Chandi Heffner out of her will because
   - ☐ a. Duke believed that Chandi was just interested in financial gain.
   - ☐ b. Duke believed that Chandi was the reincarnation of her dead daughter.
   - ☐ c. Chandi tried to poison Duke.

5. At the end of her life, Duke's closest friend was
   - ☐ a. her dance teacher.
   - ☐ b. her butler, Bernard Lafferty.
   - ☐ c. Norbu Chen.

Score 5 points for each correct answer.

_____ **Total Score:** Recalling Facts

C | Making Inferences

When you combine your own experience and information from a text to draw a conclusion that is not directly stated in that text, you are making an inference. Below are five statements that may or may not be inferences based on information in the article. Label the statements using the following key:

C—Correct Inference   F—Faulty Inference

_____ 1. Doris Duke trusted her father more than she trusted her mother.

_____ 2. Duke's loss of her baby caused the breakup of her first marriage.

_____ 3. Everyone Duke knew was just interested in her money.

_____ 4. The methods Duke used to find happiness were all tried and true.

_____ 5. Bernard Lafferty cared for Duke in the final months of her life because he was a true friend.

Score 5 points for each correct answer.

_____ **Total Score:** Making Inferences

D | Using Words Precisely

Each numbered sentence below contains an underlined word or phrase from the article. Following the sentence are three definitions. One definition is closest to the meaning of the underlined word. One definition is opposite or nearly opposite. Label those two definitions using the following key. Do not label the remaining definition.

C—Closest   O—Opposite or Nearly Opposite

1. In the end, though, Duke's life illustrated an old cliché: Money can't buy happiness.

_____ a. unusual expression

_____ b. old suspicion

_____ c. familiar saying

2. So again and again he told her to be wary.

_____ a. cruel

_____ b. careful

_____ c. reckless

3. On her wedding day, she had the groom sign a prenuptial agreement, which prevented him from ever getting control of her money.

_____ a. after the wedding ceremony

_____ b. before the wedding ceremony

_____ c. legally binding

4. She attended lavish parties.

_____ a. foreign

_____ b. economical

_____ c. extravagant

5. She thought everybody was after her money, <u>lamented</u> one acquaintance.

_____ a. moaned

_____ b. rejoiced

_____ c. confirmed

_____ Score 3 points for each correct C answer.

_____ Score 2 points for each correct O answer.

_____ Total Score: Using Words Precisely

Enter the four total scores in the spaces below, and add them together to find your Reading Comprehension Score. Then record your score on the graph on page 73.

Score	Question Type	Lesson 4
_____	Finding the Main Idea	
_____	Recalling Facts	
_____	Making Inferences	
_____	Using Words Precisely	
_____	**Reading Comprehension Score**	

Author's Approach

Put an X in the box next to the correct answer.

1. The author uses the first sentence of the article to

☐ a. inform the reader about Doris Duke's wealth.

☐ b. entertain the reader with a list of everything that Doris Duke owned.

☐ c. compare Doris Duke's penthouse in New York City with her mansion in Hawaii.

2. What is the author's purpose in writing "Doris Duke: Poor Little Rich Girl"?

☐ a. To express an opinion about rich people

☐ b. To inform the reader about Doris Duke's unhappy life

☐ c. To emphasize the similarities between rich people and poor people

3. Which of the following statements from the article best describes Doris Duke's inner thoughts?

☐ a. "As a baby, Doris was carried around on a silk pillow."

☐ b. "She handled her money so well that by the time she died, she was worth well over one billion dollars."

☐ c. "She wanted to form a deeper connection to people, but her suspicions got in the way."

4. What does the author imply by saying "At age 14, one year after her father died, she sued her mother to gain control of some of her inheritance"?

☐ a. Duke hated her mother.

☐ b. Duke didn't even trust her own mother.

☐ c. Duke loved her father only for his money.

_____ Number of correct answers

Record your personal assessment of your work on the Critical Thinking Chart on page 74.

Summarizing and Paraphrasing

Follow the directions provided for questions 1 and 2. Put an X in the box next to the correct answer for question 3.

1. Look for the important ideas and events in paragraphs 5 and 6. Summarize those paragraphs in one or two sentences.

_____

_____

_____

2. Complete the following one-sentence summary of the article using the lettered phrases from the phrase bank below. Write the letters on the lines.

> **Phrase Bank:**
> a. her death as a lonely old woman
> b. her father's deathbed advice
> c. how her distrust destroyed her life

The article about Doris Duke begins with _____, goes on to explain _____, and ends with _____.

3. Read the statement about the article below. Then read the paraphrase of that statement. Choose the reason that best tells why the paraphrase does not say the same thing as the statement.

Statement: Doris Duke traveled all over the world and bought whatever she wanted, but happiness and inner peace still eluded her.

Paraphrase: Duke forgot her cares when she traveled and acquired new possessions.

☐ a. Paraphrase says too much.

☐ b. Paraphrase doesn't say enough.

☐ c. Paraphrase doesn't agree with the statement about the article.

_____ Number of correct answers

Record your personal assessment of your work on the Critical Thinking Chart on page 74.

Critical Thinking

Follow the directions provided for questions 1, 3, and 4. Put an X in the box next to the correct answer for the other question.

1. For each statement below, write O if it expresses an opinion and write F if it expresses a fact.

_____ a. All the men Doris Duke dated were after her money.

_____ b. Duke's suspicious nature drove many of her friends away.

_____ c. Norbu Chen was the reincarnation of Tibet's Dalai Lama.

2. From the article, you can predict that if Duke's daughter Arden had lived,

☐ a. she would not have inherited the Duke fortune.

☐ b. Duke would have abandoned her eventually.

☐ c. Duke would have taught her to distrust people.

3. Choose from the letters below to correctly complete the following statement. Write the letters on the lines.

In the article, _____ and _____ are alike.

a. Doris Duke's attitude toward people

b. James Duke's attitude toward people

c. Eduardo Tirella's attitude toward people

4. Read paragraph 14. Then choose from the letters below to correctly complete the following statement. Write the letters on the lines.

According to paragraph 14, _____ happened because _____.

a. Duke's daughter died soon after birth

b. Duke became convinced that Cromwell valued only her money

c. Cromwell asked for a $7 million settlement

_____ Number of correct answers

Record your personal assessment of your work on the Critical Thinking Chart on page 74.

Personal Response

I know how Doris Duke felt because

_____

_____

_____

_____

Self-Assessment

I can't really understand how

_____

_____

_____

_____

JOHNNY APPLESEED
Planting the Wilderness

Illustration of John "Johnny Appleseed" Chapman by F. Davis

John Chapman wasn't what you'd call a snappy dresser. In fact, he often dressed in old coffee sacks and walked around with a pan tied to his head. Even during the frontier days of the United States, when settlers lived a rough and simple life, he was quite a sight.

2 In the early 1800s, pioneer families often spotted Johnny trudging across snowy fields or following the banks of a river. He slept on the ground and ate whatever nuts or berries he could find. A light traveler, he carried only two sacks with him. The smaller one held all his possessions. The larger one contained hundreds of thousands of apple seeds. Those apple seeds are what earned him the nickname Johnny Appleseed.

3 Johnny began planting apple seeds in 1801. He was 26 years old at the time, and eager to help extend the western boundary of the United States. To most people, extending the frontier meant moving out to the Midwest and settling down to live in Indiana, Michigan, or Ohio. It meant building homes, schools, and roads. It meant battling hostile Indians and stalking wild game. But Johnny Appleseed did not think or act like other people. He wanted to pave the way

for settlers by planting apple trees. Johnny believed the presence of the fruit-bearing trees would make life easier for settlers. The fragrance of the blossoms would lift the spirits of weary pioneers. The beauty of the trees would be a living symbol of God's love, he thought. In addition, the apples would have practical uses. Settlers could make applesauce, apple pies, apple dumplings, and apple butter. They could make apple vinegar as a preservative for vegetables. And they could make apple brandy.

4 Armed with only his good intentions and his sack full of seeds, he set out for the western wilderness. For 50 years he wandered the frontier, digging little holes and dropping in apple seeds. He did try settling down from time to time, and often spent winters with his sister's family in Ohio. But sooner or later he would get restless. So he would take off again, his bag of seeds slung over his shoulder. On each trip, he tried to plant as many seeds as possible. Sometimes he fenced off two or three acres of land and planted a small orchard. He liked to return to those orchards every few years to check on the progress of the saplings.

5 His journeys afforded him plenty of time to study nature. And the more he studied it, the more he loved it. In fact,

Johnny got a little carried away. He got so he couldn't bear the thought of harming any living creature. If he saw a bug heading toward his campfire, he quickly doused the flames to save the insect. He even worried that the smoke from his fire might choke an innocent mosquito. One

time he accidentally stepped on a worm. When he realized what he had done, a look of horror spread across his face. After mourning the death of the worm, he decided to punish that killer foot of his. He headed for a path strewn with sharp stones. Then he took off his shoe and

A cider mill, used for making apple cider, set up in an apple orchard, 1903

made the offending foot walk barefoot for several miles.

6   Clearly, a man like Johnny wouldn't consider eating meat or wearing clothes made of animal skin or fur. He also refused to ride a horse because he felt that that would be cruel to the animal. In fact, he regularly came to the aid of old, broken-down horses. He couldn't stand to see them abused or turned loose to die in the forests, so he bought them, raising the necessary money by doing odd jobs. Then he persuaded friends to care for them while he continued his travels. Johnny showed equal concern for the health and comfort of his apple trees. Although he picked apples, he could never bring himself to prune a branch.

7   Naturally, most people thought Johnny was a little weird. They wondered aloud if perhaps he had been kicked in the head by a horse. He had, as one man described it, a "thick bark of queerness on him." Still, people had to admire his toughness. If his shoes wore out in the middle of winter, he didn't care. He just kept walking over the icy ground until he found a pair that some settler had discarded. If he hurt himself, he would treat the wound by burning it with a hot piece of iron. As painful as that method was, it did seal the wound. Then Johnny merely had to deal with a third-degree burn.

8   Johnny always felt completely at ease in the wilderness. He thought of bears and wolves and poisonous snakes as his friends. He didn't worry about Indians, either. He treated all Indians with such gentleness that they never dreamed of harming him. According to legend, Johnny was so relaxed that he could fall asleep anywhere. It is said that he once dozed off in his canoe and didn't wake up until he had drifted a hundred miles downstream. On another occasion, a group of Seneca Indians mistook him for an enemy and began chasing him. As the story goes, Johnny slipped into a swamp and lay down so that only his mouth was above water. Then he drifted peacefully off to sleep, waking up long after the warriors had passed.

9   In 1844, at the age of 70, Johnny Appleseed was still going strong. Then, in March of 1845, he made his last journey.

Hearing that cattle had broken down one of his orchard fences, he set out on a 15-mile hike through the snow to repair it. Along the way he caught pneumonia. Johnny Appleseed died a few days later. The trees he had planted remained a monument to him, forming the core of many of the country's best and most beautiful orchards. 🍃

If you have been timed while reading this article, enter your reading time below. Then turn to the Words-per-Minute Table on page 71 and look up your reading speed (words per minute). Enter your reading speed on the graph on page 72.

Reading Time: Lesson 5

_____ : _____
Minutes   Seconds

A | Finding the Main Idea

One statement below expresses the main idea of the article. One statement is too general, or too broad. The other statement explains only part of the article; it is too narrow. Label the statements using the following key:

M—Main Idea   **B—Too Broad**   **N—Too Narrow**

_____ 1. Johnny Appleseed planted thousands of apple trees in the Midwest.

_____ 2. Johnny Appleseed lived a wandering life.

_____ 3. Johnny Appleseed loved and respected all of nature, and traveled the frontier planting apple seeds.

_____ Score 15 points for a correct M answer.

_____ Score 5 points for each correct B or N answer.

_____ **Total Score:** Finding the Main Idea

B | Recalling Facts

How well do you remember the facts in the article? Put an X in the box next to the answer that correctly completes each statement about the article.

1. Johnny Appleseed did not eat
   - ☐ a. meat.
   - ☐ b. apples.
   - ☐ c. vegetables.

2. Johnny often spent winters with
   - ☐ a. the Seneca Indians.
   - ☐ b. friends in Boston, Massachusetts.
   - ☐ c. his sister's family in Ohio.

3. Johnny bought old, broken-down
   - ☐ a. shoes.
   - ☐ b. horses.
   - ☐ c. fences.

4. Johnny treated his wounds by
   - ☐ a. burning them with a hot piece of iron.
   - ☐ b. soaking them in swamp water.
   - ☐ c. rubbing apple juice into them.

5. The last trip Johnny took was a
   - ☐ a. 15-mile hike through the snow.
   - ☐ b. horseback ride over the mountains.
   - ☐ c. journey to visit his sister.

Score 5 points for each correct answer.

_____ **Total Score:** Recalling Facts

C Making Inferences

When you combine your own experience and information from a text to draw a conclusion that is not directly stated in that text, you are making an inference. Below are five statements that may or may not be inferences based on information in the article. Label the statements using the following key:

C—Correct Inference   F—Faulty Inference

_____ 1. No one in Johnny's family ate meat or wore clothes made from animal skins.

_____ 2. Johnny Appleseed was basically lazy.

_____ 3. It is likely that Johnny Appleseed planted more apple trees than anyone else in his day.

_____ 4. Pruning branches will kill an apple tree.

_____ 5. Johnny Appleseed didn't feel that personal appearance was of great importance.

Score 5 points for each correct answer.

_____ **Total Score:** Making Inferences

D Using Words Precisely

Each numbered sentence below contains an underlined word or phrase from the article. Following the sentence are three definitions. One definition is closest to the meaning of the underlined word. One definition is opposite or nearly opposite. Label those two definitions using the following key. Do not label the remaining definition.

C—Closest   O—Opposite or Nearly Opposite

1. If he saw a bug heading toward his campfire, he quickly <u>doused</u> the flames to save the insect from a painful burn.

_____ a. lit

_____ b. watched

_____ c. extinguished

2. He headed for a path <u>strewn with</u> sharp stones.

_____ a. empty of

_____ b. covered with

_____ c. destroyed by

3. He just kept walking over the icy ground until he found another pair that some settler had <u>discarded</u>.

_____ a. used

_____ b. thrown away

_____ c. picked up

4. His journeys <u>afforded</u> him plenty of time to study nature.

_____ a. provided

_____ b. sold

_____ c. denied

5. Then he took off his shoe and made the <u>offending</u> foot walk barefoot for several miles.

_____ a. guilty

_____ b. painful

_____ c. innocent

_____ Score 3 points for each correct C answer.

_____ Score 2 points for each correct O answer.

_____ **Total Score:** Using Words Precisely

Enter the four total scores in the spaces below, and add them together to find your Reading Comprehension Score. Then record your score on the graph on page 73.

Score	Question Type	Lesson 5
_____	Finding the Main Idea	
_____	Recalling Facts	
_____	Making Inferences	
_____	Using Words Precisely	
_____	**Reading Comprehension Score**	

Author's Approach

Put an X in the box next to the correct answer.

1. What does the author mean by the statement "They wondered aloud if perhaps he had been kicked in the head by a horse"?

   ☐ a. People thought that Johnny Appleseed was crazy.

   ☐ b. People worried that one of his horses had attacked him.

   ☐ c. People wanted to know more about Johnny.

2. What is the author's purpose in writing "Johnny Appleseed: Planting the Wilderness"?

   ☐ a. To encourage the reader to be kinder to animals

   ☐ b. To inform the reader about Johnny Appleseed's life and achievements

   ☐ c. To entertain the reader with a description of Johnny Appleseed's ridiculous beliefs

3. From the statements below, choose those that you believe the author would agree with.

   ☐ a. Johnny Appleseed would never willingly hurt a fly.

   ☐ b. Johnny Appleseed was a crazy man who ruined the wilderness.

   ☐ c. Johnny Appleseed took better care of plants and animals than he did of himself.

4. Choose the statement below that best describes the author's position in paragraph 8.

   ☐ a. Johnny was always very tired as a result of his constant traveling.

   ☐ b. Johnny was a very gentle and calm person.

   ☐ c. Johnny was an excellent swimmer.

_____ Number of correct answers

Record your personal assessment of your work on the Critical Thinking Chart on page 74.

CRITICAL THINKING

CRITICAL THINKING

Summarizing and Paraphrasing

Follow the directions provided for question 1. Put an X in the box next to the correct answer for question 2.

1. Look for the important ideas and events in paragraphs 3 and 4. Summarize those paragraphs in one or two sentences.

_____

_____

_____

2. Choose the best one-sentence paraphrase for the following sentence from the article:

   "He couldn't stand to see horses abused or turned loose to die in the forests, so he bought them, raising the necessary money by doing odd jobs."

   ☐ a. He used the horses he rescued to do some odd jobs and make a little extra money.

   ☐ b. He raised the money to buy abused horses and then turned them loose in the forest.

   ☐ c. He bought abused and abandoned horses with the money he had made doing odd jobs.

_____ Number of correct answers

Record your personal assessment of your work on the Critical Thinking Chart on page 74.

Critical Thinking

Put an X in the box next to the correct answer.

1. Which of the following statements from the article is an opinion rather than a fact?

   ☐ a. "Johnny began planting apple seeds in 1801."

   ☐ b. "In fact, Johnny got a little carried away."

   ☐ c. A man like Johnny wouldn't consider eating meat or wearing clothes made of animal skin or fur.

2. From the article, you can predict that if a mosquito bit Johnny,

   ☐ a. he would walk barefoot for several miles.

   ☐ b. he would swat at it.

   ☐ c. he wouldn't harm it.

3. What was the effect of Johnny's decision to repair an orchard fence in March 1845?

   ☐ a. He slipped into a swamp.

   ☐ b. He drifted peacefully off to sleep.

   ☐ c. He caught pneumonia and died.

4. How is Johnny Appleseed an example of an eccentric?

   ☐ a. He lived according to his own set of principles.

   ☐ b. He never ate meat.

   ☐ c. He could fall asleep anywhere.

5. What did you have to do to answer question 1?

☐ a. find an opinion (what someone thinks about something)

☐ b. find a fact (something that you can prove is true)

☐ c. find an effect (something that happened)

_____ Number of correct answers

Record your personal assessment of your work on the Critical Thinking Chart on page 74.

Self-Assessment

Before reading this article, I already knew

_____

_____

_____

_____

Personal Response

If you could ask the author of the article one question, what would it be?

_____

_____

_____

_____

DIAMOND JIM BRADY
Man with the Boundless Appetite

"If you're going to make money, you have to look like money." James Buchanan Brady said it, and he believed every word. Brady, a 19th-century millionaire, liked to show off his fancy clothes. He acquired a vast wardrobe that included 200 custom-made suits and 50 silk hats. Mostly, though, Brady loved diamonds. He felt that a man without diamonds was a man without power.

2   Brady believed that diamonds impressed people, and he wanted to impress. He carried a handful of diamonds around in his pocket. No one in New York City ever saw larger diamond rings than the ones Brady wore. He even had an enormous diamond set in the top of his cane. He wore diamond cuff links and diamond shirt studs and diamond watches. He once bought his girlfriend a gold-plated bicycle and had a string of diamonds embedded in the handlebars. Brady never apologized for his extravagant spending habits. And he gloried in his well-earned nickname, Diamond Jim.

3   Brady didn't start out in life surrounded by diamonds. He grew up in a

Diamond Jim Brady loved fine things. This photo shows the opulent interior of Diamond Jim's house.

poor working-class section of New York City. As a boy, he worked in his father's saloon. But young Brady loathed the saloon. In 1867, at the age of 11, he ran away from home. Within a few years, he got a job selling equipment for the New York Central Railroad. It seemed that Brady could sell anything to anyone. Before reaching the age of 30, he had amassed a sizable fortune. He could afford anything he wanted. He could buy diamonds and fine clothes, and he could eat in all the best restaurants.

4   If Brady had a weakness for diamonds, he had an even greater weakness for food. He just may have been the all-time American eating champion. His appetite knew no bounds. After fleeing his father's saloon, young Brady first went to work at New York's St. James Hotel as a bellhop. Free food came with the job. But Brady ate so much that the hotel made a new rule. Jim Brady could not eat at the employees' free lunch bar.

5   Later, as a wealthy man, Diamond Jim could eat all he wanted. And he ate enough to kill most people. In fact, some of his friends wondered why he didn't drop dead in the middle of one of his colossal meals. Take a look at his typical breakfast: he began with a large steak, pork chops, and a plateful of eggs. Then

he downed a stack of pancakes, fried potatoes, corn bread, and a half dozen muffins. He washed everything down with a pitcher of milk and a gallon of orange juice. This breakfast he viewed as a light snack just to get him going. He saved his serious eating for later in the day.

6   Around 11:30 in the morning, Diamond Jim liked to snack on two or three dozen oysters. He insisted on having oysters every day. During the summer, he often stayed at the Manhattan Beach Hotel in New York. After breakfast, Diamond Jim would go for a swim in the pool. The hotel waiters would watch to see when he came out of the water. Then they would scurry around madly to get a huge platter of chilled, freshly opened oysters ready by the time Brady set foot on the hotel porch.

7   At 12:30 every day, Brady had lunch. His usual fare included two broiled lobsters, more oysters, and deviled crabs. That part of the meal would be followed up by a large steak and a few pieces of fruit pie. For dessert, Diamond Jim would consume a two-pound box of chocolates. He said that the chocolates helped to settle his stomach.

8   In just two meals, Diamond Jim had eaten enough food to keep the average person going for a week. But everything

Note the diamond pin in Diamond Jim's tie.

he had consumed to that point was just a warm-up for dinner. Diamond Jim often dined at Charles Rector's in New York City. The owner once boasted that Brady was "the best 25 customers" he had. People who saw Diamond Jim eat dinner would swear that he ate like a man who hadn't seen food in weeks.

9   Diamond Jim especially loved seafood. He usually began dinner with around 30 oysters. Then he would feast on a half dozen crabs before wolfing down two bowls of green turtle soup. Only then would he move on to the main courses. An average Brady dinner included six lobsters, a couple of ducks, steak, and vegetables. Diamond Jim followed that with a tray full of pastries and his customary two-pound box of chocolates. As usual, he washed down his banquet with several quarts of orange juice. He never drank coffee, tea, or alcohol.

10   Brady clearly liked large quantities of food. But he didn't go for bulk alone; he prized high-quality treats. Once he sampled a box of chocolates from Page and Shaw, a small Boston candymaker. Claiming it was the best candy he had ever tasted, Diamond Jim ordered several hundred boxes for himself and his friends.

The candymakers, however, couldn't fill the order. Their plant was too small. Without a pause, Diamond Jim wrote out an interest-free loan for $150,000. He told the candymakers to double the size of their plant. They could repay him with chocolates.

11   On another occasion, Diamond Jim became obsessed with a fish sauce he had tried in Paris. Only one restaurant in the world made it, and the recipe was a closely guarded secret. But Charles Rector wanted nothing more than to please his favorite customer. So he took his son out of law school and sent him to Paris to steal the recipe.

12   Under an assumed name, the young man got a job washing pots at the Paris restaurant. Slowly he worked his way up to assistant chef. It took him several months, but he finally got the recipe. When his boat arrived back in New York, Charles Rector and Diamond Jim were waiting anxiously at the pier. Before the boat had even docked, Brady shouted up to young Rector, "Have you got the sauce?"

13   The three men quickly drove to Charles Rector's. That night Diamond Jim fully indulged himself. He polished off

nine plates of fish smothered in the sauce. Satisfied at last, he turned to Charles Rector and said, "If you poured some of the sauce over a Turkish towel, I believe I could eat all of it."

14   Diamond Jim's eating habits finally caught up with him. He developed serious stomach problems. His days as a fabled eater came to an end. He died in 1917 at the age of 61. After his death, doctors discovered that his stomach had stretched to six times the size of a normal stomach.

If you have been timed while reading this article, enter your reading time below. Then turn to the Words-per-Minute Table on page 71 and look up your reading speed (words per minute). Enter your reading speed on the graph on page 72.

Reading Time: Lesson 6

_____ : _____
Minutes   Seconds

A | Finding the Main Idea

One statement below expresses the main idea of the article. One statement is too general, or too broad. The other statement explains only part of the article; it is too narrow. Label the statements using the following key:

M—Main Idea   **B—Too Broad**   **N—Too Narrow**

_____ 1. Diamond Jim Brady had a great love for diamonds and an even greater love for food.

_____ 2. Diamond Jim Brady was a 19th-century millionaire who lived in New York City.

_____ 3. Diamond Jim Brady lived a life of excess.

_____ Score 15 points for a correct M answer.

_____ Score 5 points for each correct B or N answer.

_____ **Total Score:** Finding the Main Idea

B | Recalling Facts

How well do you remember the facts in the article? Put an X in the box next to the answer that correctly completes each statement about the article.

1. Jim Brady made his fortune by
   - ☐ a. owning and running fine restaurants.
   - ☐ b. selling railroad equipment.
   - ☐ c. running a saloon.

2. Diamond Jim never drank
   - ☐ a. milk.
   - ☐ b. orange juice.
   - ☐ c. alcohol.

3. Charles Rector's son went to Paris to
   - ☐ a. steal the recipe for a special fish sauce.
   - ☐ b. open a candy store.
   - ☐ c. buy rare French coffee beans.

4. The St. James Hotel refused to let Brady
   - ☐ a. eat at the employees' free lunch bar.
   - ☐ b. pay for the meals he ate there.
   - ☐ c. wear his diamond rings in the dining room.

5. After Brady's death, doctors learned that his stomach had
   - ☐ a. been filled with cancer.
   - ☐ b. stretched to six times its normal size.
   - ☐ c. a tapeworm in it.

Score 5 points for each correct answer.

_____ **Total Score:** Recalling Facts

C | Making Inferences

When you combine your own experience and information from a text to draw a conclusion that is not directly stated in that text, you are making an inference. Below are five statements that may or may not be inferences based on information in the article. Label the statements using the following key:

C—Correct Inference   **F—Faulty Inference**

_____ 1. Though Jim Brady ate a lot, he ate a balanced diet.

_____ 2. Jim Brady worried constantly about his health.

_____ 3. Jim Brady found great wealth impressive.

_____ 4. Diamond Jim spent a lot of money in Charles Rector's restaurant.

_____ 5. By the time of his death, Jim Brady had no money left.

Score 5 points for each correct answer.

_____ **Total Score:** Making Inferences

D | Using Words Precisely

Each numbered sentence below contains an underlined word or phrase from the article. Following the sentence are three definitions. One definition is closest to the meaning of the underlined word. One definition is opposite or nearly opposite. Label those two definitions using the following key. Do not label the remaining definition.

C—Closest   **O—Opposite or Nearly Opposite**

1. Before reaching the age of 30, he had <u>amassed</u> a sizable fortune.

_____ a. spent

_____ b. accumulated

_____ c. stolen

2. His appetite knew no <u>bounds</u>.

_____ a. shame

_____ b. total freedom

_____ c. limits

3. In fact, some of his friends wondered why he didn't drop dead in the middle of one of his <u>colossal</u> meals.

_____ a. expensive

_____ b. enormous

_____ c. tiny

4. Diamond Jim followed that with a tray full of pastries and his <u>customary</u> two-pound box of chocolates.

_____ a. usual

_____ b. rare

_____ c. heavy

5. That night Diamond Jim fully <u>indulged</u> himself.

_____ a. gave in to desires

_____ b. sickened

_____ c. denied

_____ Score 3 points for each correct C answer.

_____ Score 2 points for each correct O answer.

_____ **Total Score:** Using Words Precisely

Enter the four total scores in the spaces below, and add them together to find your Reading Comprehension Score. Then record your score on the graph on page 73.

Score	Question Type	Lesson 6
_____	Finding the Main Idea	
_____	Recalling Facts	
_____	Making Inferences	
_____	Using Words Precisely	
_____	**Reading Comprehension Score**	

Author's Approach

Put an X in the box next to the correct answer.

1. The main purpose of the first paragraph is to

☐ a. describe Jim Brady's philosophy.

☐ b. inform the reader about Jim Brady's wardrobe.

☐ c. emphasize the importance of diamonds to powerful men.

2. Which of the following statements from the article best describes Jim Brady's personal habits?

☐ a. "He grew up in a poor working-class section of New York City."

☐ b. "It seemed that Brady could sell anything to anyone."

☐ c. "He just may have been the all-time American eating champion."

3. In this article, "The owner once boasted that Brady was 'the best 25 customers' he had" means

☐ a. Brady was more generous than most people.

☐ b. Brady always ate with a large group of people.

☐ c. Brady could eat as much as 25 people.

_____ Number of correct answers

Record your personal assessment of your work on the Critical Thinking Chart on page 74.

Summarizing and Paraphrasing

Follow the directions provided for question 1. Put an X in the box next to the correct answer for the other questions.

1. Look for the important ideas and events in paragraphs 11 and 12. Summarize those paragraphs in one or two sentences.

_____

_____

_____

2. Below are summaries of the article. Choose the summary that says all the most important things about the article but in the fewest words.

☐ a. Jim Brady ate enormous breakfasts, lunches, and dinners.

☐ b. Jim Brady had the money to indulge his enormous appetite and buy all the high-quality treats he desired.

☐ c. Jim Brady ate more at one meal than most people ate in a week. A typical dinner included seafood, soup, meats, vegetables, pastries, and chocolates.

3. Choose the sentence that correctly restates the following sentence from the article:

"Then the waiters would scurry around madly to get a huge platter of chilled, freshly opened oysters ready by the time Brady set foot on the hotel porch."

☐ a. The waiters drove themselves crazy trying to prepare Brady's lunch.

☐ b. The waiters competed to see who could get Brady's oysters ready first.

☐ c. The waiters rushed to have Brady's oysters ready to eat as soon as he appeared on the patio.

_____ Number of correct answers

Record your personal assessment of your work on the Critical Thinking Chart on page 74.

Critical Thinking

Follow the directions provided for questions 1 and 3. Put an X in the box next to the correct answer for the other questions.

1. For each statement below, write O if it expresses an opinion and write F if it expresses a fact.

_____ a. Brady loved to eat.

_____ b. Brady ran away from home at the age of 11.

_____ c. In Brady's day, a man without diamonds was a man without power.

CRITICAL THINKING

2. From what the article told about Jim Brady, you can predict that

☐ a. he would not allow anything to prevent him from buying something he really wanted.

☐ b. he would eat great quantities of low-quality food.

☐ c. he would spend thousands of dollars on fine wines.

3. Choose from the letters below to correctly complete the following statement. Write the letters on the lines.

On the positive side, _____ but on the negative side _____.

a. Jim Brady enjoyed eating

b. Jim Brady had a weakness for diamonds

c. Jim Brady developed serious stomach problems

4. What was the cause of the rule at the St. James Hotel that prevented Brady from receiving free food?

☐ a. Brady was just a bellhop.

☐ b. Brady ate too much.

☐ c. Brady ran away from his father's saloon.

5. In which paragraph did you find your information or details to answer question 4?

_____

Personal Response

I can't believe

_____

_____

_____

_____

Self-Assessment

I can't really understand how

_____

_____

_____

_____

_____ Number of correct answers

Record your personal assessment of your work on the Critical Thinking Chart on page 74.

CRITICAL THINKING

LILLIE HITCHCOCK COIT
Chasing Fire Engines

Lillie Hitchcock Coit was an honorary member of the Knickerbocker Engine Company, No. 5 in San Francisco.

Lillie Hitchcock Coit would not be an eccentric if she were alive today. She would be a firefighter, and that would be the end of the story. Lillie, however, was born in the 19th century, when women were not supposed to take up such daring careers. Since she could not be a firefighter, Lillie did the next best thing—she chased fire engines. In her day, that made her a full-blown eccentric.

2   In 1851, when Lillie was seven, she and her family moved from Maryland to San Francisco. Not long after that, Lillie had her first encounter with fire. She and some friends were playing in a vacant house. Suddenly, for reasons unknown, a fire broke out. Lillie managed to get out just in time. Two of her friends didn't. Lillie had a surprising reaction to the tragedy. Rather than making her afraid, it seemed to give Lillie an odd fascination with fire.

3   Lillie had plenty of chances to indulge that fascination. She grew up in an era when most buildings were made of wood. There were no sprinklers or fire alarms, so fires were a real menace. Hilly, windy, and mostly unpaved, San Francisco was

especially prone to lethal fires. People called it a "tinderbox town." Six times in the 1800s, major conflagrations wiped out huge sections of the city.

4   There were no motorized fire engines at this time. All fire engines had two ropes tied onto their front end so they could be pulled by hand. By the time the men pulled their engine up some steep hill, there was a fair chance that the building would already have burned to the ground. Worse, the fire might have spread to other buildings.

5   Still, the city's firefighters did their best. They were all volunteers, mostly from the upper class—bankers, doctors, lawyers, and merchants. When the alarm rang, they dropped what they were doing and rushed to their engines. Although the work was dangerous, it did have a certain glamour. The people of San Francisco treated the firefighters like heroes. And the men looked pretty sharp in their red shirts, black caps and pants, and shining black boots.

6   The city's 14 fire companies were a bit like today's sports teams. They competed against each other to see who could get to a fire first. Crowds followed the engines and cheered on their favorites. At night, young boys often raced ahead of the engines with lighted torches.

7   The symbol for the fastest company was a foxtail. If one engine passed another, the foxtail had to be turned over to the faster company. That company kept the foxtail until another company's engine passed its engine by. Once in a while, the competition got so fierce that fights broke out between the fire companies. Then the firefighters spent a night in jail.

8   Like everyone else, young Lillie admired these firefighters. One day, as legend has it, Lillie was heading home from school. She saw her favorite company—Knickerbocker Engine Company No. 5—struggling to get to a fire. For some reason, the company didn't have enough men that day. Lillie saw they needed help. So she dropped her books and grabbed one of the tow ropes.

9   She then shouted to other bystanders to pitch in. As she tugged on the rope, Lillie yelled, "Come on, you men. Beat the other engines to the top!" One man, shaking his head, shouted back, "It's not my funeral." But when others saw the little girl pulling on the rope, they joined in. As a result, No. 5 won the race to douse the fire.

10   From then on, Lillie seemed to be at every fire. Whenever a blaze was spotted from a lookout on top of Telegraph Hill,

an alarm bell was rung a certain number of times. Each section of town had its own number of rings. The number told the firefighters where to go. Lillie learned the

Construction of the Coit Tower in San Francisco

alarm code. So she was often able to beat all the engines to a fire.

11 After Lillie had helped Engine No. 5 several more times, the men adopted her as their lucky "mascot." They gave her an honorary uniform and a gold firefighter's badge which read "No. 5." Although Lillie would one day become rich, this badge would remain her proudest possession. She wore it everywhere. And for the rest of her life, she always wrote the number *5* after her name.

12 Lillie took a lot of teasing from members of the rival companies. At one fire, a firefighter from No. 6 taunted, "Well, look at the sissy member of No. 5."

13 "Sissy nothing," replied one of the men from No. 5. "She can take it."

14 To prove it, he turned his hose on Lillie, soaking her and her new dress. Lillie just laughed.

15 "What did I tell you?" chuckled the No. 5 firefighter. "She's one of the boys."

16 For the next 30 years, Lillie chased fire engines and loved every minute of it. Lillie often took the men out to eat at a fine restaurant after a fire. She also joined the men when they smoked cigars and played poker all night. Lillie's eccentric behavior amused most of the city. But her mad pranks didn't please her father or—after she married—her husband.

17 In 1863, Lillie became the wife of Benjamin Howard Coit. Their marriage was not a good match. Coit was a wealthy businessman. He enjoyed hobnobbing with the upper crust of society and wore only the finest clothes. Lillie often embarrassed him with her outrageous acts.

18 When Coit objected to her habit of chasing fire engines, Lillie decided to show him she could be wild in other ways, too. She bleached her hair a freakish shade of yellow. Coit was angry, but Lillie didn't back down. Instead, she shaved her head and began wearing black, red, and blond wigs. Desperate to change her, Coit took her on a cruise around the world. When they returned home, however, Lillie went right back to seeing her pals at Engine No. 5.

19 At that point, Lillie's father stepped in. He bought Lillie an estate miles from the city. He thought moving her to the country might keep her out of trouble. But Lillie found a way to bring her quiet new home to life. She turned the estate into a retreat for offbeat artists and writers.

20 In 1885, Lillie's husband died. Lillie then moved to France, where she spent most of the rest of her life. She came back to San Francisco in the 1920s and died there at the age of 86. She was cremated wearing her No. 5 badge, so that the metal melted into her ashes.

21 Lillie had no children. In her will, she left two-thirds of her money to the universities of Maryland and California. The last third she gave to the city of San Francisco. She asked that it be used to "[add] to the beauty of the city which I have always loved." The money was used to build Coit Tower on Telegraph Hill. This seven-story tower is a memorial to the city's firefighters. Today it is one of the most famous landmarks in the city. More than 200,000 people visit the tower every year. To most people, the outside of the tower looks like a giant fire hose. That would have pleased Lillie Hitchcock Coit very much.

If you have been timed while reading this article, enter your reading time below. Then turn to the Words-per-Minute Table on page 71 and look up your reading speed (words per minute). Enter your reading speed on the graph on page 72.

Reading Time: Lesson 7

_____ : _____
Minutes   Seconds

A Finding the Main Idea

One statement below expresses the main idea of the article. One statement is too general, or too broad. The other statement explains only part of the article; it is too narrow. Label the statements using the following key:

M—Main Idea   **B—Too Broad**   **N—Too Narrow**

_____ 1. A childhood fascination with fire led Lillie Hitchcock Coit to chase fire engines and spend much of her time with a company of San Francisco firefighters.

_____ 2. Fires plagued San Francisco in the 1800s because most buildings were made of wood.

_____ 3. Lillie Hitchock Coit often smoked cigars and played poker with the firefighters after they had put out a fire.

_____ Score 15 points for a correct M answer.

_____ Score 5 points for each correct B or N answer.

_____ **Total Score:** Finding the Main Idea

B Recalling Facts

How well do you remember the facts in the article? Put an X in the box next to the answer that correctly completes each statement about the article.

1. In the 1800s, fire engines were pulled by
   ☐ a. hand.
   ☐ b. horses.
   ☐ c. motors.

2. When a fire broke out, crowds of people
   ☐ a. ran away from the blaze.
   ☐ b. gave foxtails to the fastest engines.
   ☐ c. followed the engines to the fire and cheered for their favorite fire companies.

3. Lillie became the mascot of her favorite fire company,
   ☐ a. Number 6.
   ☐ b. Number 5.
   ☐ c. Number 8.

4. When Lillie's husband objected to her habit of chasing fire engines, Lillie
   ☐ a. stopped her eccentric behavior.
   ☐ b. moved into a quiet country estate.
   ☐ c. became even wilder.

5. After she died, Lillie was cremated wearing her firefighter's
   ☐ a. badge.
   ☐ b. hat.
   ☐ c. uniform.

Score 5 points for each correct answer.

_____ **Total Score:** Recalling Facts

C | Making Inferences

When you combine your own experience and information from a text to draw a conclusion that is not directly stated in that text, you are making an inference. Below are five statements that may or may not be inferences based on information in the article. Label the statements using the following key:

C—Correct Inference   **F—Faulty Inference**

_____ 1. Lillie did not care what other people thought of her.

_____ 2. Benjamin Coit shared Lillie's fascination with fire and firefighters.

_____ 3. The firefighters in Engine No. 5 resented Lillie's intrusion into their lives and their work.

_____ 4. Lillie left San Francisco and moved to France because she had come to hate the city.

_____ 5. Even as an old woman, Lillie recalled her experiences with engine company No. 5 with great fondness.

Score 5 points for each correct answer. _____ **Total Score:** Making Inferences

D | Using Words Precisely

Each numbered sentence below contains an underlined word or phrase from the article. Following the sentence are three definitions. One definition is closest to the meaning of the underlined word. One definition is opposite or nearly opposite. Label those two definitions using the following key. Do not label the remaining definition.

C—Closest   **O—Opposite or Nearly Opposite**

1. She and some friends were playing in a <u>vacant</u> house.

_____ a. full

_____ b. dirty

_____ c. empty

2. Hilly, windy, and mostly unpaved, San Francisco was especially prone to <u>lethal</u> fires.

_____ a. healthful

_____ b. deadly

_____ c. accidental

3. Six times in the 1800s, major <u>conflagrations</u> wiped out huge sections of the city.

_____ a. tiny sparks

_____ b. large blazes

_____ c. terrible fights

4. As a result, No. 5 won the race to <u>douse</u> the fire.

_____ a. arrive at

_____ b. ignite

_____ c. extinguish

5. <u>Desperate</u> to change her, Coit took her on a cruise around the world.

_____ a. unconcerned

_____ b. unable

_____ c. anxious

_____ Score 3 points for each correct C answer.

_____ Score 2 points for each correct O answer.

_____ **Total Score:** Using Words Precisely

Enter the four total scores in the spaces below, and add them together to find your Reading Comprehension Score. Then record your score on the graph on page 73.

Score	Question Type	Lesson 7
_____	Finding the Main Idea	
_____	Recalling Facts	
_____	Making Inferences	
_____	Using Words Precisely	
_____	**Reading Comprehension Score**	

Author's Approach

Put an X in the box next to the correct answer.

1. What does the author mean by the statement "Lillie Hitchcock Coit would not be an eccentric if she were alive today"?

☐ a. Women today can do what they want without being considered eccentric.

☐ b. Women today do so many strange things that Lillie would not seem particularly eccentric.

☐ c. Lillie's behavior would not be considered eccentric today because many people are fascinated by fire.

2. The main purpose of the first paragraph is to

☐ a. inform the reader about the condition of women in the 19th century.

☐ b. describe firefighters in the 19th century.

☐ c. explain why Lillie was considered eccentric.

3. From the statements below, choose those that you believe the author would agree with.

☐ a. Lillie's outrageous behavior should have been discouraged by the members of Knickerbocker Engine Company No. 5.

☐ b. Lillie's father should have praised his daughter for her willingness to help the firefighters.

☐ c. Lillie should not have married Benjamin Howard Coit.

CRITICAL THINKING

4. In this article, "People called it a 'tinderbox town'" means that

☐ a.   San Francisco had frequent fires.

☐ b.   the houses in San Francisco were very small.

☐ c.   San Francisco had more fire engine companies than other cities.

_____ Number of correct answers

Record your personal assessment of your work on the Critical Thinking Chart on page 74.

Summarizing and Paraphrasing

Follow the directions provided for question 1. Put an X in the box next to the correct answer for question 2.

1. Reread paragraph 18 in the article. Below, write a summary of the paragraph in no more than 25 words.

_____

_____

_____

_____

Reread your summary and decide if the summary covers important parts of the paragraph. Next, decide how to shorten the summary to 15 words or less without leaving out any essential information. Write this summary below.

_____

_____

_____

2. Choose the best one-sentence paraphrase for the following sentence from the article:

"After Lillie had helped Engine No. 5 several more times, the men adopted her as their lucky 'mascot.'"

☐ a.   The men of No. 5 adopted Lillie after her father disowned her.

☐ b.   Because Lillie had helped the men of No. 5 so much, she became their good luck charm.

☐ c.   The only reason the men of No. 5 liked Lillie was because she brought them good luck.

_____ Number of correct answers

Record your personal assessment of your work on the Critical Thinking Chart on page 74.

Critical Thinking

Put an X in the box next to the correct answer for questions 1, 2, and 5. Follow the directions provided for the other questions.

1. Which of the following statements from the article is an opinion rather than a fact?

☐ a.   More than 200,000 people visit the tower every year.

☐ b.   Lillie Hitchcock Coit would not be an eccentric if she were alive today.

☐ c.   In 1863, Lillie became the wife of Benjamin Howard Coit.

2. Judging by Lillie Hitchcock Coit's actions as described in this article, you can predict that

☐ a.   she would have set a fire just to see the firefighters rush to the scene of the blaze.

☐ b.   she would have moved to France years before if she hadn't married Benjamin Coit.

☐ c.   she would have joined Engine No. 5 as a real firefighter if such a thing had been allowed.

3. Choose from the letters below to correctly complete the following statement. Write the letters on the lines.

   On the positive side, _____, but on the negative side _____.

   a. her family did not approve of her behavior

   b. Lillie moved to San Francisco when she was seven

   c. Lillie did what she wanted

4. Read paragraph 3. Then choose from the letters below to correctly complete the following statement. Write the letters on the lines.

   According to paragraph 3, _____ because _____.

   a. the buildings were made of wood and there were no sprinklers or fire alarms

   b. fires were common in San Francisco

   c. San Francico's streets were not paved

5. What did you have to do to answer question 2?

   ☐ a. find an opinion (what someone thinks about something)

   ☐ b. find a cause (why something happened)

   ☐ c. make a prediction (what might happen next)

   _____ Number of correct answers

   Record your personal assessment of your work on the Critical Thinking Chart on page 74.

Personal Response

A question I would like answered by Lillie Hitchcock Coit is

_____

_____

_____

_____

Self-Assessment

One of the things I did best when reading this article was

_____

_____

_____

_____

I believe I did this well because

_____

_____

_____

_____

CRITICAL THINKING

Compare and Contrast

Think about the articles you have read in Unit One. Pick the four eccentrics you think were the most unusual. Write the titles of the articles that tell about them in the first column of the chart below. Use information you learned from the articles to fill in the empty boxes in the chart.

Title	Which habits or actions of this person did you find most remarkable?	How did the people around this person react to his or her eccentricities?	How do you feel about this person? Would you be more likely to praise or ridicule him or her? Why?

The eccentric I would most like to meet is _____. I chose this person because _____

_____

_____

Words-per-Minute Table

Unit One

Directions: If you were timed while reading an article, refer to the Reading Time you recorded in the box at the end of the article. Use this words-per-minute table to determine your reading speed for that article. Then plot your reading speed on the graph on page 72.

Lesson No. of Words	Sample 924	1 824	2 1092	3 816	4 1155	5 985	6 1117	7 1228	
1:30	616	549	728	544	770	657	745	819	**90**
1:40	554	494	655	490	693	591	670	737	**100**
1:50	504	449	596	445	630	537	609	670	**110**
2:00	462	412	546	408	578	493	559	614	**120**
2:10	426	380	504	377	533	455	516	567	**130**
2:20	396	353	468	350	495	422	479	526	**140**
2:30	370	330	437	326	462	394	447	491	**150**
2:40	347	309	410	306	433	369	419	461	**160**
2:50	326	291	385	288	408	348	394	433	**170**
3:00	308	275	364	272	385	328	372	409	**180**
3:10	292	260	345	258	365	311	353	388	**190**
3:20	277	247	328	245	347	296	335	368	**200**
3:30	264	235	312	233	330	281	319	351	**210**
3:40	252	225	298	223	315	269	305	335	**220**
3:50	241	215	285	213	301	257	291	320	**230**
4:00	231	206	273	204	289	246	279	307	**240**
4:10	222	198	262	196	277	236	268	295	**250**
4:20	213	190	252	188	267	227	258	283	**260**
4:30	205	183	243	181	257	219	248	273	**270**
4:40	198	177	234	175	248	211	239	263	**280**
4:50	191	170	226	169	239	204	231	254	**290**
5:00	185	165	218	163	231	197	223	246	**300**
5:10	179	159	211	158	224	191	216	238	**310**
5:20	173	155	205	153	217	185	209	230	**320**
5:30	168	150	199	148	210	179	203	223	**330**
5:40	163	145	193	144	204	174	197	217	**340**
5:50	158	141	187	140	198	169	191	211	**350**
6:00	154	137	182	136	193	164	186	205	**360**
6:10	150	134	177	132	187	160	181	199	**370**
6:20	146	130	172	129	182	156	176	194	**380**
6:30	142	127	168	126	178	152	172	189	**390**
6:40	139	124	164	122	173	148	168	184	**400**
6:50	135	121	160	119	169	144	163	180	**410**
7:00	132	118	156	117	165	141	160	175	**420**
7:10	129	115	152	114	161	137	156	171	**430**
7:20	126	112	149	111	158	134	152	167	**440**
7:30	123	110	146	109	154	131	149	164	**450**
7:40	121	107	142	106	151	128	146	160	**460**
7:50	118	105	139	104	147	126	143	157	**470**
8:00	116	103	137	102	144	123	140	154	**480**

Minutes and Seconds

Seconds

Plotting Your Progress: Reading Speed

Unit One

Directions: If you were timed while reading an article, write your words-per-minute rate for that article in the box under the number of the lesson. Then plot your reading speed on the graph by putting a small X on the line directly above the number of the lesson, across from the number of words per minute you read. As you mark your speed for each lesson, graph your progress by drawing a line to connect the X's.

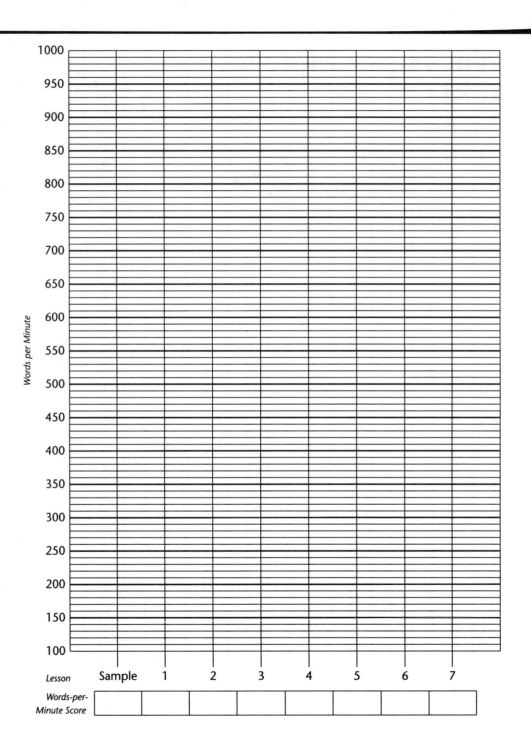

Lesson	Sample	1	2	3	4	5	6	7
Words-per-Minute Score								

Plotting Your Progress: Reading Comprehension

Unit One

Directions: Write your Reading Comprehension score for each lesson in the box under the number of the lesson. Then plot your score on the graph by putting a small X on the line directly above the number of the lesson and across from the score you earned. As you mark your score for each lesson, graph your progress by drawing a line to connect the X's.

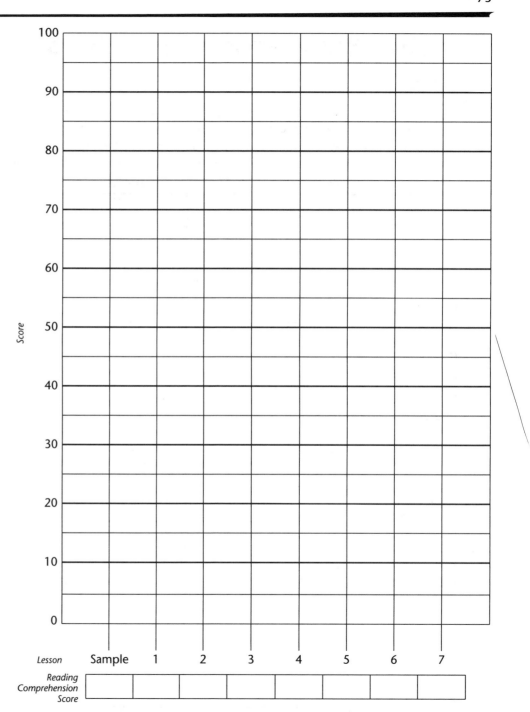

Score

100
90
80
70
60
50
40
30
20
10
0

| Lesson | Sample | 1 | 2 | 3 | 4 | 5 | 6 | 7 |

Reading Comprehension Score

Plotting Your Progress: Critical Thinking

Unit One

Directions: Work with your teacher to evaluate your responses to the Critical Thinking questions for each lesson. Then fill in the appropriate spaces in the chart below. For each lesson and each type of Critical Thinking question, do the following: Mark a minus sign (–) in the box to indicate areas in which you feel you could improve. Mark a plus sign (+) to indicate areas in which you feel you did well. Mark a minus-slash-plus sign (–/+) to indicate areas in which you had mixed success. Then write any comments you have about your performance, including ideas for improvement.

Lesson	Author's Approach	Summarizing and Paraphrasing	Critical Thinking
Sample			
1			
2			
3			
4			
5			
6			
7			

UNIT TWO

BILL VEECK
Entertaining the Fans

"For the Browns, number one-eighth, Eddie Gaedel, batting for Saucier."

The public address announcer said it, but no one could believe it. The umpire certainly didn't believe it. He took one look at Gaedel and stormed over to the Browns' dugout, demanding to know what was going on. When he found out, he tried his best not to laugh. Gaedel had a perfectly legal major league baseball contract. The three-foot seven-inch midget really planned to pinch hit for center fielder Frank Saucier of the St. Louis Browns.

2   Bobby Cain, pitcher for the Detroit Tigers, looked at Gaedel in disbelief. The St. Louis fans roared with delight. How could Cain throw strikes to a midget? Well, he couldn't. He threw Gaedel four straight high pitches, walking him. Another player immediately went out to first base to run in Gaedel's place. Gaedel simply jogged off the field to the cheers of the fans, never again to appear in a major league baseball game. Bill Veeck (pronounced VEK), the owner of the St. Louis Browns, had pulled off another shameless stunt.

Bill Veeck (left) and player Charley Grimm strike up a tune for baseball fans before a Brewers game.

3   Baseball writers across the country let Veeck know what they thought of his latest gimmick. Some called it "shameful," "cheap," and a "mockery of the sport." Joe Williams, a writer for the *New York World-Telegram*, wrote, "What Veeck calls showmanship can more often be accurately identified as vulgarity." The next day, August 20, 1951, the American League barred midgets from major league baseball. Will Harridge, president of the American League, then tried to wipe Eddie Gaedel's name from the record book. But Veeck, who had promised baseball immortality to his small friend, raised a storm of protest. He reminded Harridge that Gaedel had a legal contract, and that the game was official. Besides, if Gaedel hadn't played, then who had batted for Saucier? Harridge quickly realized that removing the midget's name from the record would be more trouble than it was worth. Gaedel's name remains in the record book to this day.

4   Bill Veeck always said that "the fan is king." He believed baseball belonged to the fans and should be fun. His way of making the game fun was to do flamboyant things to entertain the folks in the stands.

5   Veeck bought his first team, the minor league Milwaukee Brewers, in 1941. The Brewers were "absolutely the worst team I had ever seen," said Veeck. Their record was 19 wins and 43 losses when he took control. When Veeck went to his first game as owner, he found exactly 22 fans in the stands. Clearly, something had to be done to draw more people into the ballpark.

6   Veeck decided to woo the public with colorful promotions. He used whatever tricks, gifts, and bargains he could think of to lure people to see the Brewers. He even organized his own jazz band to entertain the fans. The band members included the team's manager, its radio announcer, its business manager, and Veeck himself. A fifth member of the band was an awful pitcher who just happened to be an excellent violin player. Veeck kept him with the team to play the violin, not to pitch. Whenever the game got a little dull, the band would wander through the stands serenading the fans.

7   Veeck also loved to give away weird door prizes. He just wanted to see how the lucky winner would react. Once he presented six live baby pigeons to the most dignified man he could find in the ballpark. Veeck wanted to see how the

Three-foot-seven-inch Ed Gaedel gets a shoe-lace assist from Zach Taylor before a Browns game in Detroit, August 21, 1951.

man would hold on to six birds while watching a ball game. The poor man gave it a good try. He lost three pigeons in the early innings, but did manage to keep the other three by holding one in each hand and the third between his knees. For being such a good sport, Veeck later sent the man a dozen fully-dressed game birds, ready for the oven.

8   On one occasion, Veeck awarded a fan the worst swaybacked horse he could find. Another fan won a dozen live lobsters, still in their cages. The lobsters spent the entire nine innings trying to crawl out of the cages. The unfortunate fan spent the time shoving them back in.

9   Veeck owned the Brewers during World War II. Wartime production kept factories open around the clock. Many women worked the night shift, seven days a week. One day a couple of female factory workers complained to Veeck that they never got to see any games because they were all played at night. So Veeck scheduled a special "Rosie the Riveter" morning game starting at 9:00 A.M. Any woman who arrived at the park wearing a hard hat or a welding mask got free admission. The ushers dressed in nightgowns and nightcaps and served free coffee and doughnuts.

10   Veeck also had some outlandish schemes for the game itself. He once installed a chicken wire screen above the right field fence. That turned the opposition's home runs into singles or doubles, as the balls bounced off the screen. Whenever the Brewers came to bat, Veeck rolled the screen out of the way. The league outlawed that practice after just one game.

11   In 1943, Veeck joined the Marines. He lost a leg during the war and had to be fitted with a wooden leg. But such a handicap could hardly slow down a man like Veeck. After the war, he got back into baseball. During his baseball career, he owned four different major league teams.

12   He never stopped dreaming up fantastic stunts to entice new fans to the ballpark. One day he gave away 20,000 orchids. Another day he presented 10,000 cupcakes to a woman just to see how much space they would occupy in her kitchen. Once, when he owned the St. Louis Browns, he even let the fans call the plays. Whenever the manager was supposed to make a major decision, Veeck held up signs suggesting possible choices. Whichever choice drew the most cheers from the crowd was what the manager would do. The Browns actually won the game.

13   During his 45-year career in baseball, Veeck managed to offend just about everyone in the game at one time or another. But he did draw people to the ballparks. And he did leave his mark on the sport. Although a couple of his teams regularly finished at the bottom, two were real winners and had tremendous fan support. In 1948, his Cleveland Indians drew over 2.6 million fans, breaking the major league attendance record. The Indians won the American League pennant and the World Series that year. On that team was Larry Doby, the first black player in the American League, whom Veeck had hired. In 1959, Veeck's Chicago White Sox won the pennant and set a club attendance record, drawing over 1.6 million fans. The great sportswriter Red Smith once wrote, "Veeck was born into baseball and belongs there."

If you have been timed while reading this article, enter your reading time below. Then turn to the Words-per-Minute Table on page 133 and look up your reading speed (words per minute). Enter your reading speed on the graph on page 134.

Reading Time: Lesson 8

_____ : _____
Minutes   Seconds

A | Finding the Main Idea

One statement below expresses the main idea of the article. One statement is too general, or too broad. The other statement explains only part of the article; it is too narrow. Label the statements using the following key:

M—Main Idea   **B—Too Broad**   **N—Too Narrow**

_____ 1. Bill Veeck, the owner of several major league baseball teams, was an outrageous character.

_____ 2. Bill Veeck used outrageous stunts to create publicity for his baseball teams and to entertain the fans.

_____ 3. Bill Veeck often got himself in trouble with baseball officials.

_____ Score 15 points for a correct M answer.

_____ Score 5 points for each correct B or N answer.

_____ **Total Score:** Finding the Main Idea

B | Recalling Facts

How well do you remember the facts in the article? Put an X in the box next to the answer that correctly completes each statement about the article.

1. Eddie Gaedel was
   ☐ a. a midget.
   ☐ b. an umpire.
   ☐ c. the owner of the Milwaukee Brewers.

2. To entertain the Milwaukee fans, Veeck organized his own
   ☐ a. bridge tournament.
   ☐ b. jazz band.
   ☐ c. boxing matches.

3. While he was in the United States Marine Corps, Veeck
   ☐ a. bought the Chicago White Sox.
   ☐ b. wrote articles for the *New York World-Telegram*.
   ☐ c. lost a leg.

4. Once Veeck gave a woman 10,000 cupcakes just to see
   ☐ a. how many of them she could eat.
   ☐ b. how much space they would take up in her kitchen.
   ☐ c. how she would hang on to them all during the game.

5. Veecks career in baseball lasted
   ☐ a. 10 years.
   ☐ b. 25 years.
   ☐ c. 45 years.

_____ **Total Score:** Recalling Facts

Score 5 points for each correct answer.

C | Making Inferences

When you combine your own experience and information from a text to draw a conclusion that is not directly stated in that text, you are making an inference. Below are five statements that may or may not be inferences based on information in the article. Label the statements using the following key:

C—Correct Inference   **F—Faulty Inference**

_____ 1. Most team owners took the game of baseball more seriously than Bill Veeck did.

_____ 2. Today midgets are allowed to play on American League baseball teams.

_____ 3. Even before he went to bat, Eddie Gaedel knew that he would get to play in only one game.

_____ 4. "Rosie the Riveter" was the nickname given to women who worked in factories during World War II.

_____ 5. Bill Veeck enjoyed losing teams more than winning teams.

Score 5 points for each correct answer.
_____ **Total Score:** Making Inferences

D | Using Words Precisely

Each numbered sentence below contains an underlined word or phrase from the article. Following the sentence are three definitions. One definition is closest to the meaning of the underlined word. One definition is opposite or nearly opposite. Label those two definitions using the following key. Do not label the remaining definition.

C—Closest   **O—Opposite or Nearly Opposite**

1. Bill Veeck, the owner of the St. Louis Browns, had pulled off another <u>shameless</u> stunt.

_____ a. respectable

_____ b. funny

_____ c. disgraceful

2. His way of making the game fun was to do <u>flamboyant</u> things to entertain the folks in the stands.

_____ a. flashy

_____ b. illegal

_____ c. conservative

3. Veeck decided to <u>woo</u> the public with colorful promotions.

_____ a. try to attract

_____ b. fool

_____ c. discourage

4. Veeck also had some <u>outlandish</u> schemes for the game itself.

_____ a. commonplace

_____ b. outrageous

_____ c. unpopular

5. He never stopped dreaming up fantastic stunts to <u>entice</u> new fans to the ballpark.

_____ a. embarrass

_____ b. lure

_____ c. repel

_____ Score 3 points for each correct C answer.

_____ Score 2 points for each correct O answer.

_____ **Total Score:** Using Words Precisely

Enter the four total scores in the spaces below, and add them together to find your Reading Comprehension Score. Then record your score on the graph on page 135.

Score	Question Type	Lesson 8
_____	Finding the Main Idea	
_____	Recalling Facts	
_____	Making Inferences	
_____	Using Words Precisely	
_____	**Reading Comprehension Score**	

Author's Approach

Put an X in the box next to the correct answer.

1. Based on the statement from the article "But such a handicap could hardly slow down a man like Veeck," you can conclude that the author wants the reader to think that

☐ a. Veeck was depressed by his war injury.

☐ b. Veeck threw himself into baseball in order to forget about his injury.

☐ c. Veeck did not let his injury get in the way of what he wanted to do.

2. What does the author imply by saying "During his 45-year career in baseball, Veeck managed to offend just about everyone in the game at one time or another"?

☐ a. Over time, just about everyone had objected to at least one of Veeck's stunts.

☐ b. Veeck's stunts always offended everyone involved in baseball.

☐ c. Veeck insulted everyone he came in contact with.

3. Choose the statement below that best explains how the author addresses the opposing point of view in the article.

☐ a. To those who object to Veeck's actions as a baseball owner, the author points out that Veeck lost a leg during World War II.

☐ b. To those who think that midgets should be barred from baseball, the author notes that Eddie successfully reached first base.

☐ c. To those who think that Veeck made a mockery of baseball, the author points out that Veeck drew new fans to the sport.

_____ Number of correct answers

Record your personal assessment of your work on the Critical Thinking Chart on page 136.

CRITICAL THINKING

Summarizing and Paraphrasing

Follow the directions provided for questions 1 and 2. Put an X in the box next to the correct answer for question 3.

1. Complete the following one-sentence summary of the article using the lettered phrases from the phrase bank below. Write the letters on the lines.

> **Phrase Bank:**
> a. a discussion of Veeck's impact on baseball
> b. Eddie Gaedel's appearance in major league baseball
> c. some of the other stunts Veeck devised to entertain and attract the fans

The article about Bill Veeck begins with _____, goes on to explain _____, and ends with _____.

2. Reread paragraph 7 in the article. Below, write a summary of the paragraph in no more than 25 words.

_____

_____

_____

_____

Reread your summary and decide if the summary covers important parts of the paragraph. Next, decide how to shorten the summary to 15 words or less without leaving out any essential information. Write this summary below.

_____

_____

_____

3. Read the statement about the article below. Then read the paraphrase of that statement. Choose the reason that best tells why the paraphrase does not say the same thing as the statement.

Statement: Bill Veeck scheduled a special morning game so that the women who worked the night shift in the wartime factories could come to the ballpark.

Paraphrase: Veeck organized a baseball game at 9:00 A.M. so that the women who worked at night in the factories during the war could come to the ballpark; those wearing a hard hat or welding mask were admitted for free.

☐ a. Paraphrase says too much.

☐ b. Paraphrase doesn't say enough.

☐ c. Paraphrase doesn't agree with the statement about the article.

> _____ Number of correct answers
>
> Record your personal assessment of your work on the Critical Thinking Chart on page 136.

Critical Thinking

Put an X in the box next to the correct answer for questions 1 and 4. Follow the directions provided for the other questions.

1. From the information in paragraph 3, you can predict that

☐ a. the National League tried to sign Eddie Gaedel to a baseball contract.

☐ b. Eddie Gaedel pinch hit for Frank Saucier in later games.

☐ c. a midget never played again in major league baseball.

CRITICAL THINKING

2. Choose from the letters below to correctly complete the following statement. Write the letters on the lines.

   In the article, _____ and _____ are alike.

   a. the Cleveland Indians' winning record under Bill Veeck

   b. the Milwaukee Brewers' winning record under Bill Veeck

   c. the Chicago White Sox's winning record under Bill Veeck

3. Choose from the letters below to correctly complete the following statement. Write the letters on the lines.

   According to the article, Bill Veeck caused _____ to _____, and the effect was _____.

   a. a chicken wire screen

   b. the opposition team's home runs were turned into singles or doubles

   c. be installed above the rightfield fence in the Brewers' ballpark

4. If you were the owner of a baseball team, how could you use the information in the article to draw fans to your games?

   ☐ a. Like Veeck, sign a midget to a major league contract.

   ☐ b. Like Veeck, make the game fun so that it would draw lots of fans.

   ☐ c. Like Veeck, install a wire screen over your rightfield fence.

   _____ Number of correct answers

   Record your personal assessment of your work on the Critical Thinking Chart on page 136.

Personal Response

Begin the first 5–8 sentences of your own article about an entertaining baseball game. It may tell of a real experience or one that is imagined.

_____

_____

_____

_____

Self-Assessment

One of the things I did best when reading this article was

_____

_____

_____

I believe I did this well because

_____

_____

_____

CRITICAL THINKING

GERTRUDE LINTZ
How "Human" Are Apes?

Gertrude Lintz helps Suzabella walk upright.

It was about 4 P.M. when Gertrude Lintz heard an ear-splitting scream coming from the barn behind her house. Her pet chimpanzee Jake had just spotted a large rat. Terrified, Jake threw himself at the door of his wooden cage. After a few tries, the 158-pound chimp broke down the door and ran out of the cage.

2   Lintz had never seen her chimp so frantic. Jake took off for the house, with Lintz following in dismay. The chimp tore through one room after another, flinging furniture and smashing lamps. When he reached the bathroom, he slammed the door and blocked it from the inside. For three hours Lintz tried to coax him out. But each time she tried to get into the bathroom, Jake threw himself at the door, shrieking wildly. At last Lintz called the police for help.

3   Fifteen policemen answered the call. They arrived at Mrs. Lintz's New York home at about 7 P.M. on July 15, 1938. After much effort, some of the officers pried open the bathroom door. Before they could grab Jake, however, he jumped out the bathroom window and escaped into a nearby tree.

4   No one could bring the chimpanzee under control. Five hours had passed since

he first saw the rat, yet he showed no signs of calming down. And so, with the permission of Gertrude Lintz, one of the officers pulled out his pistol and shot Jake dead.

5 As far as the policemen were concerned, the whole affair was a bizarre but isolated episode. When they went back to the station, they knew they wouldn't have to think about chimpanzees again for a long time. For Gertrude Lintz, though, chimpanzees were part of everyday life. And the killing of one signified a major failure.

6 Gertrude Lintz was a wealthy woman married to a New York doctor. During the 1920s and 1930s, she and her husband lived on a grand estate in New York City. In those days, most doctors' wives spent their days at museums or opera houses. Lintz went in a different direction. She followed the great scientific debate of her time closely. That debate was about evolution. Many people thought the theory of evolution was absurd. In 1925, a schoolteacher in Tennessee was put on trial for teaching the theory to his students. The resulting trial—called the Scopes Monkey Trial—captured national attention.

7 Gertrude Lintz thought the uproar was ridiculous. To her, the truth was perfectly clear. Humans and apes clearly came from the same evolutionary tree. A gorilla, she said, was "a child of the human stem." To prove her point, Lintz decided to take some apes into her home. She planned to raise them in as human a setting as possible. That way she could demonstrate just how "human" they really were.

8 Lintz's plan was not a scientific one. It was more an expression of love. The woman absolutely adored animals. She had quite a menagerie at her house already. She owned dogs, rabbits, horses, and kittens. She had guinea pigs, fish, pigeons, and geese. She took in hedgehogs, raccoons, owls, and snakes. She even owned a leopard.

9 Into that mix came four chimpanzees and two gorillas. Today it would be impossible for anyone to keep a gorilla as a pet, but in those days there were no regulations about such things. Lintz had talked to a friend of hers who was a sea captain. She had arranged for him to bring her the animals she wanted.

10 Lintz did her best to raise the six apes as if they were human children. She dressed them in human clothing, trained them to walk on their hind feet, and made them do chores around the house. She taught them proper table manners. When they got sick, she treated them the way any mother would treat a sick child— she fed them chicken soup.

11 For a while, Lintz's scheme seemed to be working. The chimps and gorillas appeared to adjust well to their New York surroundings. The chimpanzees could sometimes be seen walking with Lintz

Massa at the Philadephia Zoo

down Fifth Avenue, dressed in white sailor suits and little white hats. Massa, one of the gorillas, grew to love his tap shoes so much that he went out of his way to find wood floors to tap across. In 1933, Lintz took Massa to the Chicago World's Fair, where he was the star of the "Gorilla Villa."

12 Soon after that, however, trouble began. The gorillas were growing up. They were getting bigger, stronger, and more temperamental. One day, Massa's wild nature finally asserted itself. Lintz and Massa were in the kitchen where Lintz had been mopping the floor. Lintz slipped on a puddle of water, and the mop went flying. When the mop handle hit Massa, the creature exploded. He attacked Lintz with a fury, sinking his teeth into her arms and legs. He stopped only when Lintz managed to grab an iron skillet and hit him over the head with it.

13 Lintz sadly faced the fact that her gorillas were not human. They needed a life different from the one she was providing. They could not be returned to the wild; they had never developed the skills needed to survive on their own. And so Gertrude Lintz sold one of her beloved gorillas to Barnum & Bailey's Circus, where he lived for 11 years. She sent the other one—Massa—to the Philadelphia Zoo, where he lived to the ripe old age of 54.

14 Lintz felt terrible about her failed experiment. Her hopes were further crushed when Jake went out of control. Still, Gertrude Lintz's efforts were not a complete loss. She proved that animals are capable of learning a great deal. She showed that the gap between humans and other animals may not be as great as some people thought. But just as important, her work showed that there are differences between humans and the other members of the animal kingdom and that those differences should be respected. 🍃

If you have been timed while reading this article, enter your reading time below. Then turn to the Words-per-Minute Table on page 133 and look up your reading speed (words per minute). Enter your reading speed on the graph on page 134.

Reading Time: **Lesson 9**

_____ : _____

Minutes   Seconds

A | Finding the Main Idea

One statement below expresses the main idea of the article. One statement is too general, or too broad. The other statement explains only part of the article; it is too narrow. Label the statements using the following key:

M—Main Idea   **B—Too Broad**   **N—Too Narrow**

_____ 1. Many people believe that apes and humans come from the same evolutionary tree.

_____ 2. Gertrude Lintz took some apes into her home to demonstrate how human they were.

_____ 3. Massa attacked Lintz after she accidentally hit him with a mop.

_____ Score 15 points for a correct M answer.

_____ Score 5 points for each correct B or N answer.

_____ **Total Score:** Finding the Main Idea

B | Recalling Facts

How well do you remember the facts in the article? Put an X in the box next to the answer that correctly completes each statement about the article.

1. Jake became so frightened by a rat that he
   - ☐ a. had to be shot by a police officer.
   - ☐ b. bit Gertrude Lintz.
   - ☐ c. had to be given to a zoo.

2. In 1925, a Tennessee school teacher was put on trial for
   - ☐ a. keeping apes in his home.
   - ☐ b. teaching the theory of evolution.
   - ☐ c. killing an ape.

3. When Lintz's six apes got sick, she
   - ☐ a. fed them chicken soup.
   - ☐ b. sold them to a circus.
   - ☐ c. dressed them in sailor suits.

4. Massa stopped biting Lintz after
   - ☐ a. she hit him with a mop handle.
   - ☐ b. he slipped in a puddle of water.
   - ☐ c. she hit him with a skillet.

5. Lintz's work proved that there are
   - ☐ a. no differences between humans and other animals.
   - ☐ b. important differences between humans and other animals.
   - ☐ c. no differences between humans and apes.

Score 5 points for each correct answer.

_____ **Total Score:** Recalling Facts

C Making Inferences

When you combine your own experience and information from a text to draw a conclusion that is not directly stated in that text, you are making an inference. Below are five statements that may or may not be inferences based on information in the article. Label the statements using the following key:

C—Correct Inference　　**F—Faulty Inference**

_____ 1. Because Lintz treated the apes like children, they loved her like a mother.

_____ 2. The apes were easier to handle when they were young.

_____ 3. Massa lived to an advanced age because Lintz had fed him chicken soup.

_____ 4. Gertrude Lintz's experiment helped change people's minds about the theory of evolution.

_____ 5. No wild animal should ever be expected to act exactly like a human.

Score 5 points for each correct answer.

_____ **Total Score:** Making Inferences

D Using Words Precisely

Each numbered sentence below contains an underlined word or phrase from the article. Following the sentence are three definitions. One definition is closest to the meaning of the underlined word. One definition is opposite or nearly opposite. Label those two definitions using the following key. Do not label the remaining definition.

C—Closest　　**O—Opposite or Nearly Opposite**

1. As far as the policemen were concerned, the whole affair was a <u>bizarre</u> but isolated episode.

_____ a. normal

_____ b. weird

_____ c. silly

2. Many people thought the theory of evolution was <u>absurd</u>.

_____ a. outdated

_____ b. reasonable

_____ c. ridiculous

3. Gertrude Lintz thought the <u>uproar</u> was ridiculous.

_____ a. commotion

_____ b. idea

_____ c. calmness

4. They were getting bigger, stronger, and more <u>temperamental</u>.

_____ a. good-natured

_____ b. moody

_____ c. well-fed

5. She proved that animals are <u>capable of</u> learning a great deal.

_____ a. powerless when it comes to

_____ b. reluctant to try

_____ c. able to succeed in

_____ Score 3 points for each correct C answer.

_____ Score 2 points for each correct O answer.

_____ **Total Score:** Using Words Precisely

Enter the four total scores in the spaces below, and add them together to find your Reading Comprehension Score. Then record your score on the graph on page 135.

Score	Question Type	Lesson 9
_____	Finding the Main Idea	
_____	Recalling Facts	
_____	Making Inferences	
_____	Using Words Precisely	
_____	**Reading Comprehension Score**	

Author's Approach

Put an X in the box next to the correct answer.

1. The author uses the first sentence of the article to

☐ a. inform the reader about the behavior of chimpanzees.

☐ b. capture the reader's attention.

☐ c. compare humans to chimpanzees.

2. In this article, "Humans and apes clearly came from the same evolutionary tree" means that

☐ a. both humans and apes once lived in trees.

☐ b. humans and apes developed in the same region.

☐ c. humans and apes are biologically related.

3. The author probably wrote this article in order to

☐ a. tell the reader about Lintz's unusual experiment.

☐ b. express an opinion about Lintz's experiment.

☐ c. emphasize the similarities between humans and apes.

_____ Number of correct answers

Record your personal assessment of your work on the Critical Thinking Chart on page 136.

CRITICAL THINKING

Summarizing and Paraphrasing

Follow the directions provided for question 1. Put an X in the box next to the correct answer for the other questions.

1. Look for the important ideas and events in paragraphs 10 and 11. Summarize those paragraphs in one or two sentences.

    _____

    _____

    _____

2. Below are summaries of the article. Choose the summary that says all the most important things about the article but in the fewest words.

    ☐ a.   Gertrude Lintz devised a plan to raise six apes as if they were human children. However, her plan failed when the apes began to assert their wild nature.

    ☐ b.   Gertrude Lintz brought six apes into her home and treated them like human children. She dressed them in clothes, made them walk on two feet, and fed them chicken soup. After several of the apes attacked her, however, Lintz abandoned her experiment and sent the animals away.

    ☐ c.   Gertrude Lintz's experiment proved that there are important differences between apes and humans.

3. Choose the sentence that correctly restates the following sentence from the article:

    "Massa, one of the gorillas, grew to love his tap shoes so much that he went out of his way to find wood floors to tap across."

    ☐ a.   Massa wore tap shoes.

    ☐ b.   Massa looked for wooden floors so that he could walk across them in his tap shoes.

    ☐ c.   Massa loved to throw his tap shoes on wooden floors and listen to the sound they made.

    _____ Number of correct answers

    Record your personal assessment of your work on the Critical Thinking Chart on page 136.

Critical Thinking

Put an X in the box next to the correct answer for questions 1 and 4. Follow the directions provided for the other questions.

1. Using the information in paragraph 14, you can predict that

    ☐ a.   Lintz did not try to raise apes in a human setting again.

    ☐ b.   Lintz continued to try raising apes in a human setting.

    ☐ c.   Lintz tried to raise other kinds of animals in a human setting.

2. Using what you know about humans and what is told about apes in the article, name three ways humans are similar to and different from apes. Cite the paragraph number(s) where you found details in the article to support your conclusions.

CRITICAL THINKING

Similarities

_____

_____

_____

Differences

_____

_____

_____

3. Choose from the letters below to correctly complete the following statement. Write the letters on the lines.

According to the article, seeing a large rat caused _____ to _____, and the effect was _____.

a. a police officer had to shoot him

b. become uncontrollable

c. the chimpanzee Jake

4. If you were an animal researcher, how could you use the information in this article?

☐ a. Like Gertrude Lintz, dress animals in human clothes.

☐ b. Like Gertrude Lintz, treat animals like human children.

☐ c. Like Gertrude Lintz, learn to respect the differences between animals and humans.

5. Which paragraphs from the article provide evidence that supports your answer to question 3?

_____

_____ Number of correct answers

Record your personal assessment of your work on the Critical Thinking Chart on page 136.

Personal Response

What was most surprising or interesting to you about this article?

_____

_____

_____

_____

Self-Assessment

One good question about this article that was not asked would be

_____

_____

_____

and the answer is

_____

_____

_____

HETTY GREEN
Money Was Everything

When Hetty Green walked through the streets of New York City in the 1880s, people stopped and stared. She wore ragged old black dresses. Her filthy hair lay matted against her head. Her hands and fingernails were encrusted with layers of dirt. She sometimes carried a tattered old handbag or a broken-down umbrella. In short, she looked like one of the most desperately poor residents of the city. But hidden in the pockets of her grimy clothes was thousands of dollars in cash and bonds. And that was only the beginning of her wealth. In fact, Hetty Green was the richest woman in the United States.

2 Hetty inherited over $1 million from her father in 1865. She inherited another million that same year from her aunt. She used her inheritance to invest in a variety of industries. Sensing that railroads were the wave of the future, she invested heavily in them. That kind of solid business sense helped her increase her fortune. By 1900, when the average American was earning $490 per year, Hetty Green's income was $7 million. Her total worth was well over $100 million.

3 Despite her wealth, Hetty hated the thought of spending money on clothes. In

Hetty Green, who was considered one of the world's richest women

fact, the thought of spending money on *anything* made her shudder. She seldom took baths because it cost a few cents to heat bath water and a few cents more to buy soap. She refused to buy a winter coat, and instead lined her clothes with newspapers to stay warm. She even carried sandwiches in her pockets so she would never have to pay restaurant prices.

4   In 1867, Hetty married a millionaire named Edward Green. What they saw in each other is hard to imagine, for they didn't share the same values. Mr. Green was a gentle, generous man who loved to travel.

5   In 1868, the Greens had a son, Edward, whom they called Ned. Three years later they had a daughter, Sylvia. The Greens never agreed on how to raise the children. Mr. Green tended to treat them kindly and buy them presents. Hetty maintained that such treatment would only spoil them. The Greens also argued about investments. Hetty never trusted her husband with money, and kept her entire fortune in accounts separate from his. As it turned out, that proved wise. In 1873, the stock market crashed, and Edward Green lost most of his money.

6   Shortly after that, the couple broke up. The children stayed with their mother. Hetty did not consider changing her stingy ways for the sake of her children.

She continued to amaze everyone with her tightfisted, penny-pinching habits. Once, for example, she misplaced a two-cent postage stamp while riding in a carriage. At the end of her journey, she refused to let the carriage leave until she found the stamp. She scoured the inside of that carriage for hours. Finally, in the middle of the night, she emerged from the carriage holding the stamp triumphantly in her hand.

7   On another occasion, she spent an entire morning rummaging through an old barn. She suspected that the barn contained things of value. When she discovered a battered sled, she knew she'd been right. The sled was in terrible condition, but it was held together by some "perfectly good nails." Hetty spent the next several hours pulling the nails out by hand. She then had a few good nails to use if she ever needed them.

8   Hetty went out of her way to save money on housing, too. Though she owned many valuable buildings, she rented them all out to others. She insisted that she and her family didn't need fancy houses. The Greens lived in a series of cheap, bug-ridden boarding houses. Often they had only one or two rooms. Naturally, Hetty thought that an icebox was a foolish luxury, as well, so their food often spoiled before it could be eaten.

9   The Greens did keep a country home in Bellows Falls, Vermont. But in 1906 the town raised the taxes on that property.

Colonel Ned Green at the wheel of a custom-made car he used to tour his estate. The car required no shifting or acceleration.

Hetty promptly boarded the place up and rarely visited it again. That didn't lower the taxes, but it did make Hetty feel good to spite the town officials.

10   At one point she rented a wretched little apartment in Hoboken, New Jersey. Soon, though, city officials notified her that her dog, Dewey, needed a license. The fee for a dog license was two dollars. Rather than pay that sum, Hetty moved out of New Jersey.

11   Hetty's stingy habits often hurt no one. But in one instance her refusal to spend money had terrible consequences. In the 1870s, her young son, Ned, injured his knee while sledding. Hetty could see that the leg was in bad shape, but she refused to take Ned to a doctor. After all, doctors charged fees for their work. So Hetty kept Ned at home and hoped the leg would heal itself. She tried the home remedy of wrapping the leg in tobacco leaves. That, of course, had no effect. The leg simply grew more and more painful. Ned began limping badly. He could no longer run or jump or play games with the other children. He lived in constant pain.

12   Finally, in 1886, his mother decided to seek help from a doctor. But she still didn't want to spend so much as a nickel to help her son. So she turned to the free clinics. She dressed Ned in his worst rags and pretended to be a beggar. Then she went from one clinic to the next, hoping to fool a doctor into providing free treatment. Unfortunately for Ned, the Greens were fairly famous by that time. Everywhere they went, doctors and nurses recognized them. At last Hetty gave up trying. She let Ned go on suffering for another two years.

13   Then, in 1888, the boy collapsed on a staircase while visiting his father. Mr. Green grew furious when he learned that Ned's leg had never received any medical attention. He immediately called in his own doctor. When the doctor saw the leg, he shook his head sadly. The tissue in the leg had decayed. The whole leg would have to be amputated. "It's too bad something wasn't done sooner," the doctor said. "Five years ago we could have saved the whole limb."

14   Rather than risk his wife's fury at having to pay a medical bill, Mr. Green scraped together the five thousand dollars for the operation himself. A surgeon cut off Ned's leg seven inches above the knee, then fitted him with a cork leg. For the rest of his life, Ned's artificial limb served as a reminder of his mother's bizarre values.

15   Hetty Green lived to be 80 years old. When she died in 1916, her body was taken to Bellows Falls, Vermont. There she received a simple burial in the cemetery of the Immanuel Episcopal Church. That surprised many people. They couldn't understand why she had chosen to be buried there. Everyone knew that Hetty Green had been raised a Quaker, not an Episcopalian, and that she had quarreled with the town over taxes. One shrewd Vermonter, however, had a simple explanation for Hetty's choice of the Immanuel graveyard. "There was free space for Hetty there," he explained.

If you have been timed while reading this article, enter your reading time below. Then turn to the Words-per-Minute Table on page 133 and look up your reading speed (words per minute). Enter your reading speed on the graph on page 134.

Reading Time: Lesson 10

_____ : _____
Minutes   *Seconds*

A | Finding the Main Idea

One statement below expresses the main idea of the article. One statement is too general, or too broad. The other statement explains only part of the article; it is too narrow. Label the statements using the following key:

M—Main Idea   **B—Too Broad**   **N—Too Narrow**

_____ 1. Although Hetty Green was the richest woman in America, she was extremely stingy.

_____ 2. Hetty Green waited so long to get medical treatment for her son's injured leg that it had to be cut off.

_____ 3. Hetty Green was an odd wealthy woman.

_____ Score 15 points for a correct M answer.

_____ Score 5 points for each correct B or N answer.

_____ **Total Score:** Finding the Main Idea

B | Recalling Facts

How well do you remember the facts in the article? Put an X in the box next to the answer that correctly completes each statement about the article.

1. By 1900 Hetty Green's wealth totaled
    ☐ a. $10 million.
    ☐ b. $100 million.
    ☐ c. $10 billion.

2. Hetty seldom took baths because she
    ☐ a. didn't like to be clean.
    ☐ b. hated to spend money for soap and hot water.
    ☐ c. was afraid she would catch a cold.

3. When the town of Bellows Falls, Vermont, raised her property taxes, Hetty promptly
    ☐ a. boarded up her house and rarely went there again.
    ☐ b. burned her house down.
    ☐ c. filed a lawsuit against the town.

4. Hetty's son, Ned, injured his knee while
    ☐ a. playing football.
    ☐ b. sledding.
    ☐ c. pulling nails out of an old sled.

5. When Hetty took her son to free clinics, she pretended to be a
    ☐ a. foreigner.
    ☐ b. doctor.
    ☐ c. beggar.

_____ Score 5 points for each correct answer.

_____ **Total Score:** Recalling Facts

C | Making Inferences

When you combine your own experience and information from a text to draw a conclusion that is not directly stated in that text, you are making an inference. Below are five statements that may or may not be inferences based on information in the article. Label the statements using the following key:

C—Correct Inference   **F—Faulty Inference**

_____ 1. Hetty Green was admired for the way she managed her money.

_____ 2. Hetty's children had happy childhoods.

_____ 3. Hetty Green's husband was not against spending money for a doctor's care.

_____ 4. Hetty would have been a nicer person if she had not had so much money.

_____ 5. After Hetty's death, Sylvia and Ned squandered their mother's fortune.

Score 5 points for each correct answer.

_____ **Total Score:** Making Inferences

D | Using Words Precisely

Each numbered sentence below contains an underlined word or phrase from the article. Following the sentence are three definitions. One definition is closest to the meaning of the underlined word. One definition is opposite or nearly opposite. Label those two definitions using the following key. Do not label the remaining definition.

C—Closest   O—Opposite or Nearly Opposite

1. 1. Hetty <u>maintained</u> that such treatment would only spoil them.

_____ a. denied

_____ b. insisted

_____ c. wrote

2. Finally, in the middle of the night, she <u>emerged from</u> the carriage holding the stamp triumphantly in her hand.

_____ a. waved at

_____ b. exited

_____ c. entered

3. That didn't lower the taxes, but it did make Hetty feel good to <u>spite</u> the town officials.

_____ a. be kind to

_____ b. annoy

_____ c. fool

4. At one point she rented a <u>wretched</u> little apartment in Hoboken, New Jersey.

_____ a. secluded

_____ b. miserable

_____ c. fine

5. One <u>shrewd</u> Vermonter, however, had a simple explanation for Hetty's choice of the Immanuel graveyard.

_____ a. clever

_____ b. mean-spirited

_____ c. dull

_____ Score 3 points for each correct C answer.

_____ Score 2 points for each correct O answer.

_____ **Total Score:** Using Words Precisely

Enter the four total scores in the spaces below, and add them together to find your Reading Comprehension Score. Then record your score on the graph on page 135.

Score	Question Type	Lesson 10
_____	Finding the Main Idea	
_____	Recalling Facts	
_____	Making Inferences	
_____	Using Words Precisely	
_____	**Reading Comprehension Score**	

Author's Approach

Put an X in the box next to the correct answer.

1. What does the author mean by the statement "For the rest of his life, Ned's artificial limb served as a reminder of his mother's bizarre values"?

☐ a. Ned's artificial leg would always remind him of his mother's great wealth.

☐ b. Ned's artificial leg would always remind him of his mother's strange appearance.

☐ c. Ned's artificial leg would always remind him of his mother's extraordinary stinginess.

2. The main purpose of the first paragraph is to

☐ a. inform the reader about Hetty Green's strange approach to money.

☐ b. compare Hetty Green to other rich women in the United States.

☐ c. describe New York City in the 1880s.

3. From the statements below, choose those that you believe the author would agree with.

☐ a. Hetty had more business sense than her husband.

☐ b. Hetty loved money more than she loved her own children.

☐ c. Ned lost his leg as a direct result of Hetty's neglect.

CRITICAL THINKING

4. How is the author's purpose for writing the article expressed in paragraph 12?

☐ a. The author informs the reader about Hetty's reputation among medical workers.

☐ b. The author tells the reader about medicine in the 1880s.

☐ c. The author describes the lengths to which Hetty was willing to go to save money.

> _____ Number of correct answers
>
> Record your personal assessment of your work on the Critical Thinking Chart on page 136.

Summarizing and Paraphrasing

Put an X in the box next to the correct answer.

1. Below are summaries of the article. Choose the summary that says all the most important things about the article but in the fewest words.

☐ a. Although she was a very wealthy woman, Hetty Green hated to spend money so much that she denied herself and her family all luxuries and even many basic necessities.

☐ b. Hetty Green was very stingy with her money.

☐ c. Hetty Green was so stingy that she did not spend money to have her son's leg treated. The injury became so severe that the boy's leg had to be amputated and he had to wear an artificial limb for the rest of his life.

2. Choose the best one-sentence paraphrase for the following sentence from the article:

"In short, she looked like one of the most desperately poor residents of the city."

☐ a. Hetty was short and very poor.

☐ b. Hetty appeared to be one of the poorest people in the city.

☐ c. Hetty searched desperately for poor people in the city.

> _____ Number of correct answers
>
> Record your personal assessment of your work on the Critical Thinking Chart on page 136.

Critical Thinking

Put an X in the box next to the correct answer for questions 1, 4, and 5. Follow the directions provided for the other questions.

1. From the article, you can predict that if Hetty's leg had been injured,

☐ a. she would have moved to another state.

☐ b. she would have sought immediate medical help.

☐ c. she would have tried to avoid paying her own medical expenses.

2. Choose from the letters below to correctly complete the following statement. Write the letters on the lines.

In the article, _____ and _____ are different.

a. Hetty Green's behavior before her marriage

b. Hetty Green's behavior after her marriage

c. Edward Green's behavior after his marriage

3. Think about cause-effect relationships in the article. Fill in the blanks in the cause-effect chart, drawing from the letters below.

Cause	Effect
Hetty's dog needed a two-dollar license.	_____
_____	The Greens' food often spoiled.
_____	Ned's leg was amputated.

   a.   Hetty refused to buy an icebox.

   b.   Hetty moved out of New Jersey.

   c.   Hetty refused to pay to have her child's injury treated.

4. Of the following theme categories, which would this story fit into?

   ☐ a.   Love conquers all.

   ☐ b.   Money isn't everything.

   ☐ c.   The best things in life are free.

5. What did you have to do to answer question 2?

   ☐ a.   find a cause (why something happened)

   ☐ b.   find a comparison (how things are the same)

   ☐ c.   find a contrast (how things are different)

_____ Number of correct answers

Record your personal assessment of your work on the Critical Thinking Chart on page 136.

Personal Response

What would you have done if you had been present when Hetty refused to have Ned's leg treated?

_____

_____

_____

_____

Self-Assessment

One good question about this article that was not asked would be

_____

_____

_____

_____

and the answer is

_____

_____

_____

_____

CRITICAL THINKING

ALAN ABEL
Professional Prankster

DEATH EXAGGERATED

Alan Abel, Satirist, Created Campaign To Clothe Animals

News of Alan Abel's death came on January 2, 1980. The *New York Times* ran a long obituary notice announcing his passing. The notice praised Abel as "a writer, musician, and film producer who specialized in satire." It went on to describe his flair for "challenging the obvious and stating the outrageous." All in all, the obituary was quite flattering. Readers were saddened to learn of this talented man's death.

2 There was only one problem. It was a total fake. Abel was alive and well and had rigged the whole thing. He had tricked the *New York Times* into believing he was dead. Two days later, the *Times* retracted the obituary and admitted its mistake.

3 Alan Abel was a trickster. He loved to pull practical jokes and even taught a course on how to do it well. He also taught a class titled "Don't Get Mad, Get Even." As Abel once remarked, "It's healthier to give ulcers than to get them."

4 Abel dreamed up his pranks in a brick-red train caboose parked in his backyard. "I find it easy to come up with nonsense," he once said. "If I'd been born five hundred years ago, I'd have been a court jester."

Professional hoaxer Alan Abel holds the newspaper account of his death.

5   Abel dedicated his life to embarrassing a few people while amusing many others. In 1959, he pulled off a classic hoax. He came up with the idea that animals should wear clothes. He declared that he was tired of seeing them run around naked. To correct the problem, he said, he was forming the Society for Indecency to Naked Animals (SINA). Abel opened an "office" on Fifth Avenue in New York City. The sign on the door looked impressive. It read: SINA National Headquarters. Abel didn't have the money to rent a real office, so he just rented the door. It was only the door to a broom closet, which he wisely kept locked.

6   Abel told people that the goal of SINA was simple. All animals, except for birds and fishes and certain very small animals, should be clothed. Said Abel, "A nude horse is a rude horse." He therefore proposed that horses be made to wear Bermuda shorts. According to SINA, naked animals threatened the welfare of children. Abel expressed outrage that children near a playground in San Francisco were exposed to unclothed animals. "There, in all their splendor, were naked rabbits, nude goats, sheep dressed only in the wool God gave them, and some chickens and ducks in nothing but feathers."

7   It was, of course, just a joke. The press played along with Abel. He appeared on CBS News, NBC's *Today Show*, and the *Tonight Show*. The *San Francisco Chronicle* published four stories on SINA. Although they were light-hearted in tone, they never exposed the movement as a farce. They gave patterns for making clothes in three sizes, including knickers for bulldogs and half-slips for cows. They instructed people on what to do if they saw a naked animal. (Throw a blanket over the animal and "call your nearest SINA chapter.") They also noted that SINA had plans underway to build a national system of animal restrooms.

8   Some people took SINA seriously. At one point, membership soared to over 50,000. Some people formed SINA local chapters and put clothes on their animals. One chapter entered a float in a Fourth of July parade. All the animals on the float were fully clothed. One woman even tried to donate $40,000 to the cause. Abel refused to take the money. He was just having fun; he wasn't trying to take money from fools.

9   In another prank, Alan Abel had his wife, Jeanne, run for president in 1964. She posed as a Bronx housewife named Yetta Bronstein. She ran as an independent. Her campaign slogan was "Vote for Yetta and Watch Things Get Better." She pledged to set up national bingo games. She also pledged to hang a suggestion box from the White House fence. Yetta didn't win. But she got lots of media attention.

10   Abel pulled off his biggest hoax in 1990. The New York state lottery had built

In 1980, Alan Abel developed a scheme to run cartoon-character Betty Boop for president.

up its jackpot to $35 million. Abel decided to create his own winner. But he didn't want a typical winner; he wanted a glamorous one. He wanted a good-looking, single woman who was very generous. Abel got some friends to help him out. One was Lee Chirillo, a pretty but unemployed actress who agreed to play the role of the lottery winner. For this stunt, Chirillo took the bogus name "Charlie Taylor."

11   To set up the hoax, Abel rented a room in a hotel in New York City. He and his friends began to party. They ordered champagne from room service. Abel then faxed the newspapers and TV stations, declaring he knew the winner. To top things off, "Ms. Taylor" began tossing money out her hotel window.

12   Some in the media waited for official word from the state lottery. Others did not. They just ran with the story. WWOR-TV ended its evening news show with this statement: "We know the winner of the $35 million Lotto jackpot; it's Charlie Taylor of Dobbs Ferry, New York." WNBC-TV proclaimed that Charlie Taylor was the single winner. The biggest sucker of all was the *New York Post*, which ran a banner headline: $35M AND SHE'S SINGLE.

13   The *Daily News* got lucky. The paper sent a reporter named Ingrid Devita to Abel's hotel. She immediately recognized Abel and called her editor. The *Daily News* headline screamed, "IT'S A HOAX." What tipped Devita off? She had once had Abel as a teacher. He had taught her a course in practical joke techniques!

14   Although his joke was now revealed, Abel claimed success. "It was beyond my wildest, craziest anticipation," he said. "When the media jumped in so fast—whew, I honestly wasn't expecting such a big blast."

15   Some of the people who fell for the hoax weren't laughing. "We've been had," said Jerry Nachman, editor of the *New York Post*. Tom Petner, of WWOR-TV, saw a potential dark side to such gags. "Maybe Alan Abel had a good yuk over this, but some day, some way, he may generate a catastrophe."

16   Why did he do it? Abel said he saw his elaborate stunts as "satire." Maybe, he suggested, people shouldn't believe everything they read. Abel didn't pull mindless jokes. As he put it, "No banana peels, no buckets of water falling on people's head, no whoopee cushions—that's low class."

17   No, Alan Abel liked to play with people's minds. "The mind is the last frontier," he once said. "I like to play, and my friends and my mind are my toys." Some people, of course, thought Abel was crazy. "Me crazy?" he laughed. "You know what I think is crazy? I think bowling is crazy—taking a ball and rolling it down the floor. That's crazy. Exploring the mind is not crazy." 🍃

If you have been timed while reading this article, enter your reading time below. Then turn to the Words-per-Minute Table on page 133 and look up your reading speed (words per minute). Enter your reading speed on the graph on page 134.

Reading Time: Lesson 11

_____ : _____
Minutes   Seconds

A | Finding the Main Idea

One statement below expresses the main idea of the article. One statement is too general, or too broad. The other statement explains only part of the article; it is too narrow. Label the statements using the following key:

M—Main Idea   **B—Too Broad**   **N—Too Narrow**

_____ 1. Alan Abel liked to pull practical jokes that played with people's minds.

_____ 2. Alan Abel dedicated his life to amusing people.

_____ 3. In one classic hoax, Alan Abel formed a society whose goal was to clothe animals.

_____ Score 15 points for a correct M answer.

_____ Score 5 points for each correct B or N answer.

_____ **Total Score:** Finding the Main Idea

B | Recalling Facts

How well do you remember the facts in the article? Put an X in the box next to the answer that correctly completes each statement about the article.

1. Abel created his pranks in a

☐ a. broom closet.

☐ b. New York City hotel room.

☐ c. brick-red train caboose.

2. When SINA was formed, the press

☐ a. played along with Abel.

☐ b. expressed outrage about the prank.

☐ c. took the society seriously.

3. In 1964, Abel's wife ran for president using the name

☐ a. Lee Chirillo.

☐ b. Yetta Bronstein.

☐ c. Ingrid Devita.

4. When Abel announced the winner of the $35 million jackpot winner,

☐ a. all the media immediately reported the story.

☐ b. no one in the media reported the story.

☐ c. some members of the media waited for confirmation of the story, while others did not.

5. Abel's elaborate stunts were designed to

☐ a. be used in scientific research of the human mind.

☐ b. cause catastrophes.

☐ c. play with people's minds.

Score 5 points for each correct answer.

_____ **Total Score:** Recalling Facts

C **Making Inferences**

When you combine your own experience and information from a text to draw a conclusion that is not directly stated in that text, you are making an inference. Below are five statements that may or may not be inferences based on information in the article. Label the statements using the following key:

C—Correct Inference   **F—Faulty Inference**

_____ 1. Alan Abel really believed that naked animals threatened the welfare of children.

_____ 2. Abel had a creative mind.

_____ 3. Abel enjoyed making people laugh.

_____ 4. Abel made a great deal of money from the people who fell for his pranks.

_____ 5. The *Daily News* is always more reliable than the *New York Post*.

Score 5 points for each correct answer.

_____ **Total Score:** Making Inferences

D **Using Words Precisely**

Each numbered sentence below contains an underlined word or phrase from the article. Following the sentence are three definitions. One definition is closest to the meaning of the underlined word. One definition is opposite or nearly opposite. Label those two definitions using the following key. Do not label the remaining definition.

C—Closest   **O—Opposite or Nearly Opposite**

1. All in all, the <u>obituary</u> was quite flattering.

_____ a. advertisement

_____ b. birth announcement

_____ c. death notice

2. It went on to describe his <u>flair</u> for challenging the obvious and stating the outrageous.

_____ a. inability

_____ b. need

_____ c. genius

3. Two days later, the *Times* <u>retracted</u> the obituary and admitted its mistake.

_____ a. maintained

_____ b. took back

_____ c. advertised

4. One woman even tried to <u>donate</u> $40,000 to the cause.

_____ a. contribute

_____ b. imagine

_____ c. withhold

5. For this stunt, Chirillo took the <u>bogus</u> name Charlie Taylor.

_____ a. unusual

_____ b. phony

_____ c. genuine

_____ Score 3 points for each correct C answer.

_____ Score 2 points for each correct O answer.

_____ **Total Score:** Using Words Precisely

Enter the four total scores in the spaces below, and add them together to find your Reading Comprehension Score. Then record your score on the graph on page 135.

Score	Question Type	Lesson 11
_____	Finding the Main Idea	
_____	Recalling Facts	
_____	Making Inferences	
_____	Using Words Precisely	
_____	**Reading Comprehension Score**	

Author's Approach

Put an X in the box next to the correct answer.

1. Which of the following statements from the article describes Alan Abel most completely?

☐ a. Abel dreamed up his pranks in a brick-red train caboose parked in his backyard.

☐ b. Abel dedicated his life to embarrassing a few people while amusing many others.

☐ c. He came up with the idea that animals should wear clothes.

2. Considering the statement from the article "He was just having fun; he wasn't trying to take money from fools," you can conclude that the author wants the reader to think that

☐ a. Abel thought all people were fools.

☐ b. Abel couldn't figure out a way to make money at other people's expense.

☐ c. Abel didn't want to hurt anyone.

3. How is the author's purpose for writing the article expressed in paragraph 17?

☐ a. The author entertains the reader with another story about Abel.

☐ b. The author tries to persuade the reader that Abel was crazy.

☐ c. The author tells the reader why Abel liked to play practical jokes.

4. The author tells this story mainly by

☐ a. comparing different pranksters.

☐ b. using his or her imagination and creativity.

☐ c. telling different stories about Alan Abel.

_____ Number of correct answers

Record your personal assessment of your work on the Critical Thinking Chart on page 136.

Summarizing and Paraphrasing

Follow the directions provided for question 1. Put an X in the box next to the correct answer for question 2.

1. Complete the following one-sentence summary of the article using the lettered phrases from the phrase bank below. Write the letters on the lines.

   Phrase Bank:
   a. Abel's reasons for playing practical jokes
   b. the description of an obituary notice announcing Abel's death
   c. some of Abel's greatest pranks

   The article about Alan Abel begins with _____, goes on to explain _____, and ends with _____.

2. Read the statement about the article below. Then read the paraphrase of that statement. Choose the reason that best tells why the paraphrase does not say the same thing as the statement.

   Statement: Although most people were amused by Abel's stunts, some people, especially those he had embarrassed, claimed that he would cause real trouble some day.

   Paraphrase: Mostly, people enjoyed Abel's pranks.

   ☐ a. Paraphrase says too much.
   ☐ b. Paraphrase doesn't say enough.
   ☐ c. Paraphrase doesn't agree with the statement about the article.

   _____ Number of correct answers

   Record your personal assessment of your work on the Critical Thinking Chart on page 136.

Critical Thinking

Put an X in the box next to the correct answer for questions 1, 2, and 4. Follow the directions provided for the other questions.

1. For each statement below, write O if it expresses an opinion and write F if it expresses a fact.

   _____ a. Abel tricked the *New York Times* into believing he was dead.

   _____ b. Many people believed that Charlie Taylor had won the $35 million lottery jackpot.

   _____ c. Alan Abel's hoaxes were funny.

2. Considering the information in paragraph 12, you can predict that

   ☐ a. the media will be more careful about checking their sources in the future.
   ☐ b. the *New York Post* will sue Alan Abel.
   ☐ c. the jackpot will be paid to Charlie Taylor.

3. Choose from the letters below to correctly complete the following statement. Write the letters on the lines.

   In the article, _____ and _____ are different people.

   a. Jeanne Abel
   b. Jerry Nachman
   c. Yetta Bronstein

4. What was the effect of Ingrid Devita's recognition of Abel?

   ☐ a. She went to Abel's hotel.
   ☐ b. She took a course from him in practical joke techniques.
   ☐ c. Her newspaper proclaimed that the jackpot story was a hoax.

5. In which paragraph did you find your information or details to answer question 4?

_____

_____

```
_____    Number of correct answers

Record your personal assessment of your work on the Critical
Thinking Chart on page 136.
```

Personal Response

This article is different from other articles about eccentrics I've read because

_____

_____

_____

_____

and Alan Abel is unlike other eccentrics because

_____

_____

_____

_____

A word or phrase in the article that I do not understand is

_____

_____

_____

_____

CRITICAL THINKING

LUDWIG II
The Dream King

Ludwig II of Bavaria painted by Ferdinand Piloty in 1865

No one ever said that King Ludwig II of Bavaria lacked a lively imagination. Once, in 1865, he had his bedroom ceiling painted with an orchard of orange trees against a blue sky. Then he commanded his servants to install an artificial moon and a rainbow. The king liked to fantasize that he was sleeping in a beautiful garden.

2   Ludwig's days were filled with fanciful illusions. So were many of his nights. Often, around 8:00 P.M., Ludwig would order a groom to bring him his horse. Pretending it was early morning, he would set off on a ride. But he never went far. For six or seven hours, the king would ride around and around the small track at the riding school. Every so often he would change horses. Ludwig imagined that he was actually going to some particular German town. In fact, he calculated the exact distance according to the circumference of the track. After a few hours in the saddle, the king would stop, and his servants would bring him a picnic supper. When Ludwig had finished his meal, he would remount his horse and continue riding in circles until he figured he had reached his "destination." After a

hard day's ride, the king would retire to his bedroom around 3:00 A.M.

3   Obviously, Ludwig had an active fantasy life. Largely for that reason, Ludwig II, who ruled Bavaria from 1864 to 1886, became known as the "Dream King."

4   When Ludwig went to his country residence, he continued his night rides. On those occasions, however, he was not constrained by a riding track. The king's wild midnight excursions became legend in the Bavarian Alps. On even the coldest winter nights, the peasants would hear sleigh bells ringing as Ludwig's golden sleigh rushed beneath their windows. The coachmen and outriders wore bright, gaudy uniforms, while Ludwig huddled in his huge fur coat.

5   Extremely shy, Ludwig did not enjoy the company of other people. In the last years of his reign, he almost always dined alone. Still, the royal servants regularly set the table for three or four people. Ludwig would imagine that he was dining with kings who lived long ago. At times he talked to those dead monarchs as if they were actually his guests.

6   Although Ludwig didn't like people, he did have a certain fondness for horses. He once invited his favorite mare to dine with him. Ludwig's servants prepared a

Neuschwanstein Castle in Bavaria, Germany

sumptuous meal of soup, fish, a roast, and wine. After the horse had eaten her share, she proceeded to smash the valuable china and crystal. Ludwig just looked on and smiled.

7   Ludwig loved the theater. But the audiences made him uncomfortable by gawking at him instead of watching the plays. So he finally insisted on private performances. The only plays that really interested him dealt with life in the French court during the 17th and 18th centuries. So he commanded the actors to perform old plays, long out of date. Ludwig even went so far as to hire local playwrights to write new plays about the French court.

8   Such eccentricities were harmless. What really got Ludwig into trouble and led to his downfall was his mania for building castles. Every king is entitled to a castle or two. But Ludwig built three in his life of only 40 years. As a child Ludwig created dream castles with toy blocks. As king he could afford to build real ones. Most kings build castles as monuments to themselves. Ludwig, however, built them as a hobby. He simply loved castles. He would dream of a certain kind of castle and then decide to build it.

9   His most famous castle, Neuschwanstein, is an elaborate fairy-tale castle perched on a mountain pinnacle. It is nearly inaccessible. A special road had to be built to reach the site. Water had to be hauled up from the valley below. In addition, twenty feet of rocky summit had to be blasted away to make enough level space for the castle. The excessive cost of Neuschwanstein and his other two castles never bothered Ludwig. Even when war broke out in 1870, work on the castle continued uninterrupted. Ludwig could withdraw from the affairs of state and live in his own private world at Neuschwanstein.

10   But the splendor of his castles could not shield the king forever. Bavaria simply couldn't afford Ludwig's boundless castle building. And the country couldn't afford to have a king who totally neglected his official duties. At last certain high officials conspired to remove Ludwig from the throne. In January 1886, they began to hatch their plot. Ludwig's uncle and heir, Prince Luitpold von Bayern, ordered doctors to declare Ludwig incurably insane and unable to rule. On January 12, the prince ordered that Ludwig be confined at Schloss Berg, a castle just outside the capital of Munich. Ludwig might have been able to fight back by rousing people in his support, for he was well loved by many of his subjects. But he continued to live in his fantasy world. He took no steps to save himself.

11   The very next day, Ludwig and his physician went for an afternoon walk down by the lake. When several hours passed and the men did not return, a couple of policemen began a search. When darkness fell, a full-scale search of the area began. About 10:00 P.M. someone spotted a black object floating in the lake. It was the king's overcoat. A half hour later, the searchers fished out the bodies of the two men. The Dream King was dead. Was it an accident? Murder? Suicide? No one knows for sure. How and why Ludwig II died remains one of the unsolved mysteries of history. 🍂

If you have been timed while reading this article, enter your reading time below. Then turn to the Words-per-Minute Table on page 133 and look up your reading speed (words per minute). Enter your reading speed on the graph on page 134.

Reading Time: Lesson 12

_____ : _____
Minutes   *Seconds*

A Finding the Main Idea

One statement below expresses the main idea of the article. One statement is too general, or too broad. The other statement explains only part of the article; it is too narrow. Label the statements using the following key:

M—Main Idea   **B—Too Broad**   **N—Too Narrow**

_____ 1. Ludwig II was a Bavarian king who had unusual ways.

_____ 2. King Ludwig II did outlandish things that interfered with his governing of Bavaria.

_____ 3. King Ludwig II often took long horseback rides to nowhere.

_____ Score 15 points for a correct M answer.

_____ Score 5 points for each correct B or N answer.

_____ **Total Score:** Finding the Main Idea

B Recalling Facts

How well do you remember the facts in the article? Put an X in the box next to the answer that correctly completes each statement about the article.

1. Ludwig was known as the
   ☐ a. Castle King.
   ☐ b. Horse King.
   ☐ c. Dream King.

2. Ludwig was very
   ☐ a. short.
   ☐ b. shy.
   ☐ c. practical.

3. Ludwig liked to pretend he was eating with
   ☐ a. monarchs who had died long ago.
   ☐ b. peasants from the Bavarian Alps.
   ☐ c. French actors.

4. Neuschwanstein was one of Ludwig's
   ☐ a. best friends.
   ☐ b. favorite mares.
   ☐ c. castles.

5. In 1886, Ludwig's uncle ordered doctors to declare Ludwig
   ☐ a. an impostor.
   ☐ b. insane.
   ☐ c. king.

Score 5 points for each correct answer.

_____ **Total Score:** Recalling Facts

C | Making Inferences

When you combine your own experience and information from a text to draw a conclusion that is not directly stated in that text, you are making an inference. Below are five statements that may or may not be inferences based on information in the article. Label the statements using the following key:

C—Correct Inference   F—Faulty Inference

_____ 1. Ludwig was a poor ruler.

_____ 2. Ludwig had many children.

_____ 3. Ludwig's castles have fallen to ruin since the Dream King's death.

_____ 4. Ludwig never ate meat.

_____ 5. Ludwig was the best-loved king in Bavarian history.

Score 5 points for each correct answer.

_____ **Total Score:** Making Inferences

D | Using Words Precisely

Each numbered sentence below contains an underlined word or phrase from the article. Following the sentence are three definitions. One definition is closest to the meaning of the underlined word. One definition is opposite or nearly opposite. Label those two definitions using the following key. Do not label the remaining definition.

C—Closest   O—Opposite or Nearly Opposite

1. Ludwig's days were filled with <u>fanciful</u> illusions.

_____ a. depressing

_____ b. realistic

_____ c. imaginative

2. On those occasions, however, he was not <u>constrained</u> by a riding track.

_____ a. held back

_____ b. released

_____ c. concerned with

3. Ludwig's servants prepared a <u>sumptuous</u> meal of soup, fish, a roast, and wine.

_____ a. magnificent

_____ b. fattening

_____ c. plain

4. His most famous castle, Neuschwanstein, is an elaborate fairy-tale castle perched on a mountain <u>pinnacle</u>.

_____ a. peak

_____ b. valley

_____ c. stream

5. It is nearly <u>inaccessible</u>. A special road had to be built to reach the site.

_____ a. easily approachable

_____ b. invisible

_____ c. unreachable

_____ Score 3 points for each correct C answer.

_____ Score 2 points for each correct O answer.

_____ **Total Score:** Using Words Precisely

Enter the four total scores in the spaces below, and add them together to find your Reading Comprehension Score. Then record your score on the graph on page 135.

Score	Question Type	Lesson 12
_____	Finding the Main Idea	
_____	Recalling Facts	
_____	Making Inferences	
_____	Using Words Precisely	
_____	**Reading Comprehension Score**	

Author's Approach

Put an X in the box next to the correct answer.

1. The author uses the first sentence of the article to
   ☐ a. inform the reader about Bavaria.
   ☐ b. describe the qualities of Ludwig's imagination.
   ☐ c. compare King Ludwig II to other Bavarian kings.

2. Judging by the statement from the article "Ludwig's uncle and heir, Prince Luitpold von Bayern, ordered doctors to declare Ludwig incurably insane and unable to rule," you can conclude that the author wants the reader to think that
   ☐ a. Ludwig was truly unfit to be king.
   ☐ b. Luitpold wanted to remove Ludwig so that he could rule.
   ☐ c. the doctors believed that Ludwig was insane.

3. What does the author imply by saying "He simply loved castles. He would dream of a certain kind of castle and then decide to build it"?
   ☐ a. Ludwig dreamed about castles only while he slept.
   ☐ b. Ludwig was an accomplished architect.
   ☐ c. Ludwig was childlike in his love of castles.

4. How is the author's purpose for writing the article expressed in paragraph 5?
   ☐ a. The author describes Ludwig's imaginary dinners with dead monarchs.
   ☐ b. The author compares Ludwig to kings who lived long ago.
   ☐ c. The author informs the reader of the dining customs in Bavaria.

_____ Number of correct answers

Record your personal assessment of your work on the Critical Thinking Chart on page 136.

CRITICAL THINKING

Summarizing and Paraphrasing

Follow the directions provided for question 1. Put an X in the box next to the correct answer for the other questions.

1. Look for the important ideas and events in paragraphs 8 and 9. Summarize those paragraphs in one or two sentences.

_____

_____

_____

2. Complete the following one-sentence summary of the article using the lettered phrases from the phrase bank below. Write the letters on the lines.

   Phrase Bank:
   a. his removal from the throne and his mysterious death
   b. his mania for building castles
   c. a description of Ludwig's fantasy life

   The article about King Ludwig II begins with _____, goes on to explain _____, and ends with _____.

3. Read the statement about the article below. Then read the paraphrase of that statement. Choose the reason that best tells why the paraphrase does not say the same thing as the statement.

   Statement: Many high officials believed that the country could no longer afford Ludwig, who neglected his duties to build fairy-tale castles.

   Paraphrase: Many high officials conspired to remove Ludwig from the throne while he was planning to build another castle.

   ☐ a. Paraphrase says too much.

   ☐ b. Paraphrase doesn't say enough.

   ☐ c. Paraphrase doesn't agree with the statement about the article.

   _____ Number of correct answers

   Record your personal assessment of your work on the Critical Thinking Chart on page 136.

Critical Thinking

Put an X in the box next to the correct answer for questions 1 and 2. Follow the directions provided for the other questions.

1. Which of the following statements from the article is an opinion rather than a fact?

   ☐ a. "He once invited his favorite mare to dine with him."

   ☐ b. "Every king is entitled to a castle or two."

   ☐ c. "The Dream King was dead."

2. From the information in paragraph 10, you can conclude that

   ☐ a. Ludwig was murdered by his physician.

   ☐ b. Ludwig and his physician both fell into the lake and drowned.

   ☐ c. Ludwig's uncle was somehow connected with his murder.

115

3. Choose from the letters below to correctly complete the following statement. Write the letters on the lines.

   On the positive side, _____, but on the negative side _____.

   a. Ludwig's castles were a drain on his country

   b. Ludwig was extremely shy

   c. Ludwig built some beautiful castles

4. Read paragraph 7. Then choose from the letters below to correctly complete the following statement. Write the letters on the lines.

   According to paragraph 7, _____ because _____.

   a. Ludwig insisted on private performances

   b. the only plays that interested him were those that dealt with life in the French court during the 17th and 18th centuries

   c. sitting with an audience made him uncomfortable

   _____ Number of correct answers

   Record your personal assessment of your work on the Critical Thinking Chart on page 136.

Personal Response

How do you think Ludwig felt when he was removed from the throne?

_____

_____

_____

_____

Self-Assessment

I'm proud of how I answered question # _____ in section _____ because

_____

_____

_____

_____

CRITICAL THINKING

SALVADOR DALI
A Question of Reality

Strange things happen in Salvador Dali's paintings. Fried eggs hang from strings. Trees grow out of pianos. Human bodies melt into violins. Horses burst from cannon barrels. Giant grasshoppers pop up everywhere, clinging to birds, boxes, human faces. What does it all mean? It is a glimpse into the artist's mind. It is Dali's contribution to surrealism.

2   Surrealism is art that explores subconscious thoughts and images. The surrealists believed that the subconscious—the inner mind—held the greatest reality. *Surreal* means "reality above reality." The surrealists created strange, dreamlike pictures to express the contents of their own subconscious minds. Dali was one of the masters of surrealism.

3   Salvador Dali's career as an artist spanned more than 60 years. Born in Spain in 1904, he began painting when he was just a young boy. In 1918 he held his first public exhibition. He went on to national and then international fame. He produced hundreds of masterpieces. At times he worked incredibly slowly. He

Salvador Dali (left) had a reputation as a great surrealist artist. He also enjoyed public antics. In the 1940s, Dali began twisting his moustache into unusual shapes, as in this picture.

once spent six months painting a still life of a loaf of bread. On other occasions, though, fantastic, dreamlike images simply welled up inside him. When that happened, Dali could work very quickly. He stated that he did not consciously create those images. He simply recorded them as they came to him. In fact, he once admitted that even he did not understand the meanings of many of them.

4   Dali was not only a painter. He pursued other creative avenues with equal flair. In the 1930s he produced stunning costumes for a ballet company. He designed eerie landscapes for the movie set of Alfred Hitchcock's famous film *Spellbound*. He wrote complex poems and essays. He designed jewelry, furniture, and clothing. He even ventured into filmmaking. His first film was a French silent movie produced in 1929. It was called *Un Chien Andalou*. Although it lasted only 17 minutes, its shocking surrealist approach made it unforgettable. It featured such powerful but violent images as a razor splitting open an eye.

5   It did not take long for Dali to earn a reputation in the art world. Everyone could see that he was a man driven by a strange inner force. It was that force that led him to produce his wild but compelling works. He never used drugs. He believed that drugs would only interfere with his attempts to capture subconscious visions. He did, however, go to great lengths to summon those visions. He believed that they would rise up within him if he was properly prepared to receive them. Once he locked himself in a small, damp room for two solid months. He kept the shutters closed the entire time, and lit the room with only one electric light bulb. He wanted to create an environment that would remind him of his mother's womb. He hoped to trigger subconscious memories of his life before birth. He would then translate the images of those memories onto canvas.

6   Dali's artistic eccentricities also exhibited themselves beyond his studio walls. He often engaged in public antics. Many resulted in front-page headlines. Perhaps he was trying to get publicity for himself and his work. Perhaps he was simply reacting to his own unique

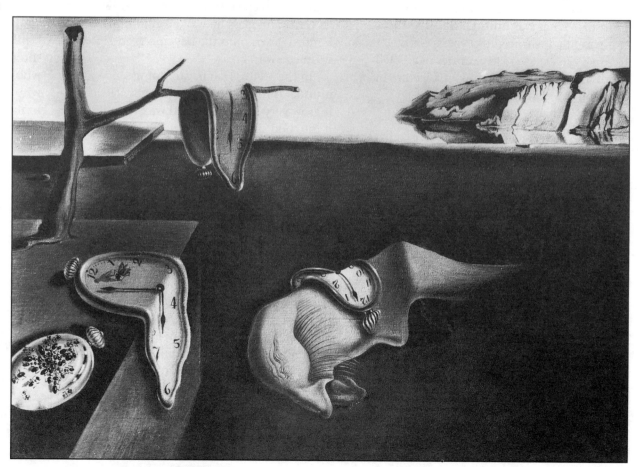

Persistence of Memory *by Salvador Dali*

perspective on the world. In any case, some of his actions became legendary.

7   Once, for instance, he greeted reporters in a strange way. He met them waving an eight-foot-long stick of bread. Another time he appeared in public wearing a tuxedo, which at first glance was unexceptional. A closer look, however, showed that he had pinned artificial flies all over the tux. For an exhibit opening in Paris, he once arrived in a Rolls-Royce. That in itself was not unusual. What was unusual was that the car was filled with cauliflower.

8   In 1936 Dali's creative antics nearly led to disaster. At the beginning of a lecture in London, he startled his audience by walking onstage in a full underwater diving suit. As he began speaking, everyone listened with great eagerness. They all hoped to gain insights into the master's work. After a few minutes, though, the audience began to look perplexed. No one could understand what Dali was saying. As he went on, his speech became more and more garbled. Soon he began making frantic gestures with his hands. Still the audience sat, unsure what it all meant. Finally some people realized what was happening. Trapped inside the airtight diver's suit, Dali could not breathe. He was suffocating before their eyes. Quickly they rushed to free him. They managed to pull off the diver's helmet just before he fainted.

9   Despite that harrowing experience, Dali continued his outrageous behavior.

In 1939 he went to New York to design a window display for a Fifth Avenue department store. The display included a fur-lined bathtub filled with water. He finished his work on the window late at night. The next morning he returned to the store to admire his creation. In the meantime, though, someone had gone in and made changes in the display. Dali was so infuriated that he climbed up into the display area and tipped over the bathtub, causing it to crash through the window. As water and glass flew all around him, he jumped down onto the pavement and stormed away.

10   In the 1940s, Dali began doing unusual things with his moustache. He let it grow very long, then used wax to mold it into odd shapes. Sometimes he twisted it into a figure eight. Sometimes he fashioned it to look like the horns of a bull. Sometimes he even dipped one end into paint and used it as a paintbrush.

11   Dali never lost his love for absurdity. By the 1980s, though, he had no strength left for zaniness. In 1982 his beloved wife Gala died. In 1984 a fire in his bedroom left him with such serious burns that he required skin grafts. After that, he went to live in seclusion in his hometown of Figueras, Spain. Dali remained in Figueras until his death in 1989. From his quarters there, he could oversee the Teatro-Museo Dali, a museum devoted to his works.

12   The museum houses many classic Dali images. It includes paintings of elephants on stilts and portraits of people with holes

cut in their chests. In one room sits an old Cadillac. It is part of a display called *Rainy Taxi*. If someone drops a coin into a slot, rain will begin falling inside the car. No guidebook is available to help viewers make sense of the art in the museum. Dali felt that each viewer had to reach his or her own conclusions about the meanings of the works.

13   For most people, it is difficult to comprehend all the messages contained within Dali's works. It is even more confusing when we take into account Dali's bizarre personal behavior. How should we assess him? Was he a genius who acted crazy? Or was he a crazy man who possessed genius? Perhaps Dali himself offered the best clue back in 1934. He said, "The only difference between myself and a madman is that I am not mad." 🍃

If you have been timed while reading this article, enter your reading time below. Then turn to the Words-per-Minute Table on page 133 and look up your reading speed (words per minute). Enter your reading speed on the graph on page 134.

Reading Time: **Lesson 13**

_____ : _____
Minutes   Seconds

A   Finding the Main Idea

One statement below expresses the main idea of the article. One statement is too general, or too broad. The other statement explains only part of the article; it is too narrow. Label the statements using the following key:

M—Main Idea   **B—Too Broad**   **N—Too Narrow**

_____ 1. Salvador Dali's life was an extension of the bizarre, dreamlike art he created.

_____ 2. Salvador Dali was an unusually imaginative twentieth-century artist.

_____ 3. At times, Salvador Dali painted slowly, and at other times images welled up inside him quickly.

_____ Score 15 points for a correct M answer.

_____ Score 5 points for each correct B or N answer.

_____ **Total Score:** Finding the Main Idea

B   Recalling Facts

How well do you remember the facts in the article? Put an X in the box next to the answer that correctly completes each statement about the article.

1. Dali spent six months working on a painting of
   - ☐ a. an elephant on stilts.
   - ☐ b. trees growing out of pianos.
   - ☐ c. a loaf of bread.

2. Dali never
   - ☐ a. used drugs.
   - ☐ b. wore a tuxedo.
   - ☐ c. created violent images.

3. Dali almost suffocated in
   - ☐ a. an underwater diving suit.
   - ☐ b. a car filled with cauliflower.
   - ☐ c. the small, damp room where he worked.

4. Dali's 1939 department store display included
   - ☐ a. ballet costumes he had designed.
   - ☐ b. an old Cadillac.
   - ☐ c. a fur-lined bathtub.

5. Dali sometimes made a figure eight out of
   - ☐ a. paintbrushes.
   - ☐ b. jewelry.
   - ☐ c. his moustache.

Score 5 points for each correct answer.

_____ **Total Score:** Recalling Facts

C | Making Inferences

When you combine your own experience and information from a text to draw a conclusion that is not directly stated in that text, you are making an inference. Below are five statements that may or may not be inferences based on information in the article. Label the statements using the following key:

C—Correct Inference   F—Faulty Inference

_____ 1. Dali preferred jewelry making to filmmaking.

_____ 2. Dali had few friends.

_____ 3. Dali enjoyed startling people.

_____ 4. Dali was better known as a filmmaker and set designer than as a painter.

_____ 5. Dali liked to attract attention to himself.

Score 5 points for each correct answer.

_____ **Total Score:** Making Inferences

D | Using Words Precisely

Each numbered sentence below contains an underlined word or phrase from the article. Following the sentence are three definitions. One definition is closest to the meaning of the underlined word. One definition is opposite or nearly opposite. Label those two definitions using the following key. Do not label the remaining definition.

C—Closest   O—Opposite or Nearly Opposite

1. On other occasions, though, fantastic, dreamlike images simply <u>welled</u> up inside him.

   _____ a. rose

   _____ b. dwindled

   _____ c. confused

2. Everyone could see that he was a man <u>driven</u> by a strange inner force.

   _____ a. pushed along

   _____ b. torn apart

   _____ c. held back

3. It was that force that led him to produce his wild but <u>compelling</u> works.

   _____ a. weak

   _____ b. forceful

   _____ c. diverse

4. Perhaps he was simply reacting to his own unique <u>perspective</u> on the world.

_____ a. viewpoint

_____ b. ignorance

_____ c. birthplace

5. By the 1980s, though, he had no strength left for <u>zaniness</u>.

_____ a. seriousness

_____ b. popularity

_____ c. kooky behavior

_____ Score 3 points for each correct C answer.

_____ Score 2 points for each correct O answer.

_____ **Total Score:** Using Words Precisely

Enter the four total scores in the spaces below, and add them together to find your Reading Comprehension Score. Then record your score on the graph on page 135.

Score	Question Type	Lesson 13
_____	Finding the Main Idea	
_____	Recalling Facts	
_____	Making Inferences	
_____	Using Words Precisely	
_____	**Reading Comprehension Score**	

Author's Approach

Put an X in the box next to the correct answer.

1. What is the author's purpose in writing "Salvador Dali: A Question of Reality"?

☐ a. To express an opinion about surrealism

☐ b. To inform the reader about Dali and his unusual view of reality

☐ c. To emphasize the similarities between Dali and a madman

2. Which of the following statements from the article best describes what Salvador Dali is best known for?

☐ a. "Born in Spain in 1904, he began painting when he was just a young boy."

☐ b. "He designed jewelry, furniture, and clothing."

☐ c. "Dali was one of the masters of surrealism."

3. In this article, "Dali's artistic eccentricities also exhibited themselves beyond his studio walls" means that

☐ a. Dali's own life reflected his appreciation of the absurd.

☐ b. Dali expressed himself through sculpture and other means.

☐ c. Dali staged many art exhibitions outside of his studio.

4. The author tells this story mainly by

☐ a. retelling other artists' experiences with Dali.

☐ b. telling different stories about Dali.

☐ c. using his or her imagination and creativity to describe Dali.

_____ Number of correct answers

Record your personal assessment of your work on the Critical Thinking Chart on page 136.

Summarizing and Paraphrasing

Follow the directions provided for question 1. Put an X in the box next to the correct answer for question 2.

1. Reread paragraph 8 in the article. Below, write a summary of the paragraph in no more than 25 words.

_____

_____

_____

_____

Reread your summary and decide whether it covers the important ideas in the paragraph. Next, decide how to shorten the summary to 15 words or less without leaving out any essential information. Write this summary below.

_____

_____

_____

2. Choose the sentence that correctly restates the following sentence from the article:

    "Dali was so infuriated that he climbed up into the display area and tipped over the bathtub, causing it to crash through the window."

    ☐ a. Dali was so mad that he jumped into the bathtub and broke the display window.

    ☐ b. Dali was so crazy that he climbed around the display, overturned the bathtub, and then crashed through the window.

    ☐ c. Dali was so angry that he overturned the bathtub, causing it to crash through the display window.

    _____ Number of correct answers

    Record your personal assessment of your work on the Critical Thinking Chart on page 136.

Critical Thinking

Follow the directions provided for questions 1 and 5. Put an X in the box next to the correct answer for the other questions.

1. For each statement below, write O if it expresses an opinion and write F if it expresses a fact.

    _____ a. Dali was a genius who acted crazy.

    _____ b. Dali was the greatest master of surrealism.

    _____ c. Dali was an artist for more than 60 years.

2. From the article, you can predict that if anyone had offered Dali suggestions for improving one of his works of art, he would have

☐ a. quit being an artist.

☐ b. ignored that person's advice.

☐ c. tried to make the suggested changes in the work.

3. What was the effect of Dali's wearing an underwater diving suit while giving a lecture?

☐ a. He nearly suffocated.

☐ b. The audience gained new insights into the master's work.

☐ c. He began doing unusual things with his moustache.

4. How is Salvador Dali an example of an eccentric?

☐ a. He did not provide guidebooks in his art museum.

☐ b. His life and art reflected his focus on absurdity.

☐ c. He never used drugs to capture subconscious visions.

5. In which paragraph did you find your information or details to answer question 3?

_____

_____ Number of correct answers

Record your personal assessment of your work on the Critical Thinking Chart on page 136.

Personal Response

What was most surprising or interesting to you about this article?

_____

_____

_____

_____

Self-Assessment

What concepts or ideas from the article were difficult to understand?

_____

_____

_____

_____

Which were easy to understand?

_____

_____

_____

_____

SUN RA
Music from Outer Space

Sun Ra, citizen of the planet Saturn, was born Herman "Sonny" Blount, citizen of Birmingham, Alabama, in 1914.

He was born Herman "Sonny" Blount in Birmingham, Alabama, in 1914. Those are the facts according to the written records. According to the man himself, though, the date, the place, and even the name are all wrong.

2   Blount maintained that he wasn't born in Birmingham at all. In fact, he said, he wasn't born anywhere on Earth. And he wasn't Sonny Blount. Rather, he was Sun Ra, a visitor from the planet Saturn. He was a bit vague about when he had first come to Earth. Perhaps it had been the year A.D. 1055. Or maybe it was a few thousand years before that.

3   Wherever he came from and whenever he arrived, the man calling himself Sun Ra was a huge hit on our planet. A piano player, composer, and bandleader, he recorded more than 125 albums. His music ranged freely from jazz to big band tunes to Tin Pan Alley and beyond. Sun Ra's eclectic music was as hard to label as he was.

4   As a child, he learned to play the piano at home. After high school, he played with a variety of bands in Alabama. Then

he started his own band, called the Sonny Blount Orchestra. The band played mostly blues, pop tunes, and a form of jazz dance music known as swing.

5 Although he was still known as Sonny Blount, he was already getting some strange visions. One night in 1935, robed figures paid him a visit in a dream. They warned him to keep inside a narrow beam of light. In other words, he should behave properly. Blount claimed these weird visitors then took him on a sightseeing trip to the planet Jupiter.

6 After that, Sonny Blount often wore a tunic and sandals. As he put it, he was now beginning to tune into "cosmic forces." He read the Bible for its "hidden meanings." He also read books on the occult. He later summed up this period by saying, "I was busy with spirit things."

7 The final transformation of Herman "Sonny" Blount occurred in 1952. On October 20 of that year, he officially changed his name to Sun Ra, a name that comes from the ancient Egyptian sun god. From that day on, Sun Ra claimed he had never been named Herman Blount. "People say I'm Herman Blount, but I don't know him," he said. "That's an imaginary person."

8 Sun Ra now told people he was a citizen of Saturn. He was not human; instead, he was from a race of angels. He had come to Earth to serve as a Cosmic Communicator. Sun Ra was here to teach humans about the Creator's message.

9 Sun Ra did everything he could to wipe out all traces of his former life. In addition to getting rid of the name Herman Blount, he changed the name of his band. Before it had been called the Space Trio; now it became the Arkestra. Whether the band's name was spelled forward or backward, it contained the letters *ra*.

A view of Saturn taken by Voyager I

10 Slowly, Sun Ra built the Arkestra into a big band. In 1956 he wrote a song titled "Saturn" in honor of his home planet. Sun Ra also started his own record company. It, too, was called Saturn. The records were homemade with hand-decorated covers. Sun Ra took a cardboard box full of these records and sold them wherever Arkestra played. All sales were cash only.

11 To see Sun Ra and the Arkestra live was a strange and wonderful sight. The band members dressed in outrageous costumes. Sometimes they wore tuxedos. Other times they donned Robin Hood outfits or capes with planets stitched onto them. They sometimes wore huge turbans or beanies with little propellers that lit up. Occasionally they appeared in white gloves with purple jackets. With Sun Ra and his band, nobody ever knew for sure what would come next.

12 Sun Ra's music, too, was frequently "out of this world." One favorite tune was "Rocket Number Nine Take-off for the Planet Venus." Others top songs included "We Travel the Spaceways," "Interplanetary Music," and "Space Loneliness." Only Sun Ra could release an album titled *My Brother the Wind, Volume II* when there was no volume one.

13 Some people loved Sun Ra's music. Others judged it too far out. Sun Ra's art, however, was always more than just music—it was also the show. And what

shows they were. One writer aptly referred to them as "sound circuses."

14 These concerts, which began in the 1950s, could be bizarre and even a bit scary. The electric sound, the light shows, and the music were all way ahead of their time. No other band was even remotely as wild as the Arkestra. At times, members of the audience were so shocked by what they experienced that they ran out of the hall.

15 Sun Ra enjoyed shocking or upsetting his fans. Before the show began he sometimes turned down the lights and left the audience in total darkness for five or six minutes. Then Sun Ra and his band would enter the room by crawling on their stomachs. All the fans could hear was the sound of bodies creeping along the aisles.

16 When the lights went on, the scene was often utter chaos. There might be all kinds of seemingly misplaced people wandering about the stage. There could be people painting at easels or carrying their paintings back and forth. There might be dancers or strong men flexing their muscles. There might even be fire-eaters, jugglers, or midgets. Bright flashing lights added to the effect. It's little wonder that some people compared Sun Ra's shows to a circus.

17 Sun Ra believed he was immortal. At least, that's what he told his fans. Since he was from Saturn and not human, he was

never going to die. (Sun Ra didn't like the idea of birth, either. If he had been born, then one day he would die. On the other hand, if he had never been born…) But, of course, the man wasn't immortal. Near the end of his life, he became very ill. Though he urged the band to keep playing, Sun Ra himself was worn out. All the performances and the touring had finally taken their toll. On May 30, 1993, at age 79, Sun Ra died. He was buried in Birmingham. At least, that's the official line. But who knows? Maybe Sun Ra is back on Saturn playing some wild music and smiling down on Earth. 🍃

If you have been timed while reading this article, enter your reading time below. Then turn to the Words-per-Minute Table on page 133 and look up your reading speed (words per minute). Enter your reading speed on the graph on page 134.

Reading Time: Lesson 14

_____ : _____

Minutes   Seconds

A Finding the Main Idea

One statement below expresses the main idea of the article. One statement is too general, or too broad. The other statement explains only part of the article; it is too narrow. Label the statements using the following key:

M—Main Idea   **B—Too Broad**   **N—Too Narrow**

_____ 1. On stage, Sun Ra and the members of his band often wore capes with planets stitched onto them.

_____ 2. Sun Ra was a musician who began performing in the 1950s.

_____ 3. Sun Ra, who claimed to have come from Saturn, was a musician whose musical style and concerts were attention getting and sometimes outrageous.

_____ Score 15 points for a correct M answer.

_____ Score 5 points for each correct B or N answer.

_____ **Total Score:** Finding the Main Idea

B Recalling Facts

How well do you remember the facts in the article? Put an X in the box next to the answer that correctly completes each statement about the article.

1. Sun Ra has claimed that he first came to Earth in
   ☐ a.   A.D. 1055.
   ☐ b.   1914.
   ☐ c.   1952.

2. When robed figures visited Sonny Blount in a dream, they took him to
   ☐ a.   Saturn.
   ☐ b.   Jupiter.
   ☐ c.   Alabama.

3. Sun Ra named himself after
   ☐ a.   the ancient Egyptian sun god.
   ☐ b.   his home planet Saturn.
   ☐ c.   Saturn's Cosmic Communicator.

4. In 1956, Sun Ra started a record company, which he called
   ☐ a.   Arkestra.
   ☐ b.   Space Trio.
   ☐ c.   Saturn.

5. Sun Ra's concerts were so wild that some members of the audience
   ☐ a.   entered the hall by crawling on their stomachs.
   ☐ b.   ran out of the hall.
   ☐ c.   wandered around the stage.

Score 5 points for each correct answer.

_____ **Total Score:** Recalling Facts

C Making Inferences

When you combine your own experience and information from a text to draw a conclusion that is not directly stated in that text, you are making an inference. Below are five statements that may or may not be inferences based on information in the article. Label the statements using the following key:

C—Correct Inference   F—Faulty Inference

_____ 1. Sun Ra was not a skilled musician.

_____ 2. Sun Ra was confident, energetic, and creative.

_____ 3. Most people believed that Sun Ra really did come from Saturn.

_____ 4. Some people went to the Arkestra's concerts just to see the show.

_____ 5. Sun Ra called his band the Arkestra because he did not know how to spell *orchestra*.

Score 5 points for each correct answer.

_____ **Total Score:** Making Inferences

D Using Words Precisely

Each numbered sentence below contains an underlined word or phrase from the article. Following the sentence are three definitions. One definition is closest to the meaning of the underlined word. One definition is opposite or nearly opposite. Label those two definitions using the following key. Do not label the remaining definition.

C—Closest   O—Opposite or Nearly Opposite

1. He was a bit <u>vague</u> about when he had first come to Earth.

_____ a. certain

_____ b. unclear

_____ c. unreasonable

2. Sun Ra's <u>eclectic</u> music was as hard to label as he was.

_____ a. drawn from many sources

_____ b. narrowly defined

_____ c. otherworldly

3. Other times they <u>donned</u> Robin Hood outfits or capes with planets stitched onto them.

_____ a. took off

_____ b. handed out

_____ c. put on

4. These concerts, which began in the 1950s, could be <u>bizarre</u> and even a bit scary.

_____ a. harmful

_____ b. weird

_____ c. ordinary

5. When the lights went on, the scene was often utter <u>chaos</u>.

_____ a. order

_____ b. horror

_____ c. confusion

_____ Score 3 points for each correct C answer.

_____ Score 2 points for each correct O answer.

_____ **Total Score:** Using Words Precisely

Enter the four total scores in the spaces below, and add them together to find your Reading Comprehension Score. Then record your score on the graph on page 135.

Score	Question Type	Lesson 14
_____	Finding the Main Idea	
_____	Recalling Facts	
_____	Making Inferences	
_____	Using Words Precisely	
_____	**Reading Comprehension Score**	

Author's Approach

Put an X in the box next to the correct answer.

1. From the statements below, choose those that you believe the author would agree with.

☐ a. Sun Ra was immortal.

☐ b. Sun Ra and his band put on spectacular concerts.

☐ c. Sun Ra was able to convince everyone that he was from Saturn.

2. Choose the statement below that is the weakest argument for believing that Sun Ra was an immortal visitor from Saturn.

☐ a. Sun Ra said that he had been taken on a sightseeing trip to Jupiter.

☐ b. Sun Ra died in 1993.

☐ c. Sun Ra's music sounded as if it came from out of this world.

3. What does the author imply by saying "He was a bit vague about when he had first come to Earth"?

☐ a. Sun Ra couldn't name a specific date because he really was from Earth.

☐ b. Sun Ra couldn't remember the actual date because he was so old.

☐ c. Sun Ra didn't think the actual date was very important.

4. Choose the statement below that best describes the author's position in paragraph 3.

☐ a. Sun Ra was popular on Earth only because he was so strange.

☐ b. Both Sun Ra and his music were unique and difficult to categorize.

☐ c. Sun Ra had trouble choosing a musical style.

_____ Number of correct answers

Record your personal assessment of your work on the Critical Thinking Chart on page 136.

CRITICAL THINKING

Summarizing and Paraphrasing

Follow the directions provided for question 1. Put an X in the box next to the correct answer for question 2.

1. Reread paragraph 17 in the article. Below, write a summary of the paragraph in no more than 25 words.

_____

_____

_____

_____

Reread your summary and decide whether it covers the important ideas in the paragraph. Next, decide how to shorten the summary to 15 words or less without leaving out any essential information. Write this summary below.

_____

_____

_____

2. Choose the sentence that correctly restates the following sentence from the article:

    "Wherever he came from and whenever he arrived, the man calling himself Sun Ra was a huge hit on our planet."

☐ a. Wherever he went, Sun Ra drew large crowds.

☐ b. Although we don't know why Sun Ra landed on Earth, he was a very popular musician.

☐ c. No matter where he came from or when he got here, Sun Ra enjoyed great popularity on Earth.

_____ Number of correct answers

Record your personal assessment of your work on the Critical Thinking Chart on page 136.

Critical Thinking

Put an X in the box next to the correct answer for questions 1, 2, 4, and 5. Follow the directions provided for the other question.

1. Which of the following statements from the article is an opinion rather than a fact?

☐ a. "He was born Herman 'Sonny' Blount in Birmingham, Alabama, in 1914."

☐ b. "On May 30, 1993, at age 79, Sun Ra died."

☐ c. "The electric sound, the light shows, and the music were all way ahead of their time."

CRITICAL THINKING

2. From what the article told about Sun Ra's popularity, you can predict that soon

☐ a. other musicians will all have forgotten him and his music.

☐ b. some fans will still remember him with appreciation.

☐ c. his band will get back together.

3. Choose from the letters below to correctly complete the following statement. Write the letters on the lines.

According to the article, _____ caused Sun Ra to _____, and the effect was _____.

a. overwork and illness

b. he eventually died

c. become worn out

4. How is Sun Ra an example of an eccentric?

☐ a. He lived and behaved unlike anyone else.

☐ b. He staged wild shows during his concerts.

☐ c. His music was hard to label.

5. What did you have to do to answer question 1?

☐ a. find a cause (why something happened)

☐ b. find a fact (something that you can prove is true)

☐ c. find an opinion (what someone thinks about something)

_____ Number of correct answers

Record your personal assessment of your work on the Critical Thinking Chart on page 136.

Personal Response

I can't believe

_____

_____

_____

Self-Assessment

1. From reading this article, I have learned

_____

_____

_____

2. The part I found most difficult about the article was

_____

_____

_____

I found this difficult because

_____

_____

_____

CRITICAL THINKING

Compare and Contrast

Think about the articles you have read in Unit Two. Pick four articles that describe the eccentrics you think are funniest or most ridiculous. Write the titles in the first column of the chart below. Use information you learned from the articles to fill in the empty boxes in the chart.

Title	What did the person do that you found funny or ridiculous?	Was anyone hurt by the actions of the eccentric? If so, who was hurt and how?	How did this eccentric break the rules?

Choose one of the eccentrics you read about. Suppose that person were alive today. Suggest at least two other activities or pranks that he or she could try.

_____

_____

Words-per-Minute Table

Unit Two

Directions: If you were timed while reading an article, refer to the Reading Time you recorded in the box at the end of the article. Use this words-per-minute table to determine your reading speed for that article. Then plot your reading speed on the graph on page 134.

Lesson / No. of Words	8 / 1147	9 / 996	10 / 1203	11 / 1146	12 / 949	13 / 1178	14 / 1075	Seconds
1:30	765	664	802	764	633	785	717	90
1:40	688	598	722	688	569	707	645	100
1:50	626	543	656	625	518	643	586	110
2:00	574	498	602	573	475	589	538	120
2:10	529	460	555	529	438	544	496	130
2:20	492	427	516	491	407	505	461	140
2:30	459	398	481	458	380	471	430	150
2:40	430	374	451	430	356	442	403	160
2:50	405	352	425	404	335	416	379	170
3:00	382	332	401	382	316	393	358	180
3:10	362	315	380	362	300	372	339	190
3:20	344	299	361	344	285	353	323	200
3:30	328	285	344	327	271	337	307	210
3:40	313	272	328	313	259	321	293	220
3:50	299	260	314	299	248	307	280	230
4:00	287	249	301	287	237	295	269	240
4:10	275	239	289	275	228	283	258	250
4:20	265	230	278	264	219	272	248	260
4:30	255	221	267	255	211	262	239	270
4:40	246	213	258	246	203	252	230	280
4:50	237	206	249	237	196	244	222	290
5:00	229	199	241	229	190	236	215	300
5:10	222	193	233	222	184	228	208	310
5:20	215	187	226	215	178	221	202	320
5:30	209	181	219	208	173	214	195	330
5:40	202	176	212	202	167	208	190	340
5:50	197	171	206	196	163	202	184	350
6:00	191	166	201	191	158	196	179	360
6:10	186	162	195	186	154	191	174	370
6:20	181	157	190	181	150	186	170	380
6:30	176	153	185	176	146	181	165	390
6:40	172	149	180	172	142	177	161	400
6:50	168	146	176	168	139	172	157	410
7:00	164	142	172	164	136	168	154	420
7:10	160	139	168	160	132	164	150	430
7:20	156	136	164	156	129	161	147	440
7:30	153	133	160	153	127	157	143	450
7:40	150	130	157	149	124	154	140	460
7:50	146	127	154	146	121	150	137	470
8:00	143	125	150	143	119	147	134	480

Minutes and Seconds

Plotting Your Progress: Reading Speed

Unit Two

Directions: If you were timed while reading an article, write your words-per-minute rate for that article in the box under the number of the lesson. Then plot your reading speed on the graph by putting a small X on the line directly above the number of the lesson, across from the number of words per minute you read. As you mark your speed for each lesson, graph your progress by drawing a line to connect the X's.

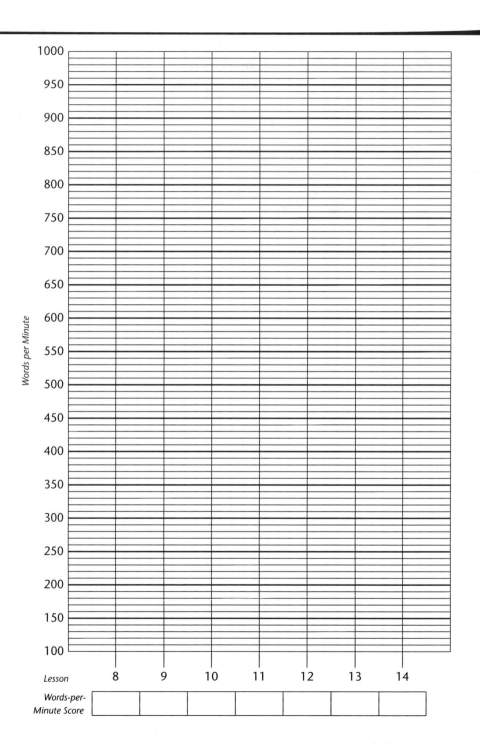

Words per Minute

Lesson   8   9   10   11   12   13   14

Words-per-Minute Score

Plotting Your Progress: Reading Comprehension

Unit Two

Directions: Write your Reading Comprehension score for each lesson in the box under the number of the lesson. Then plot your score on the graph by putting a small X on the line directly above the number of the lesson and across from the score you earned. As you mark your score for each lesson, graph your progress by drawing a line to connect the X's.

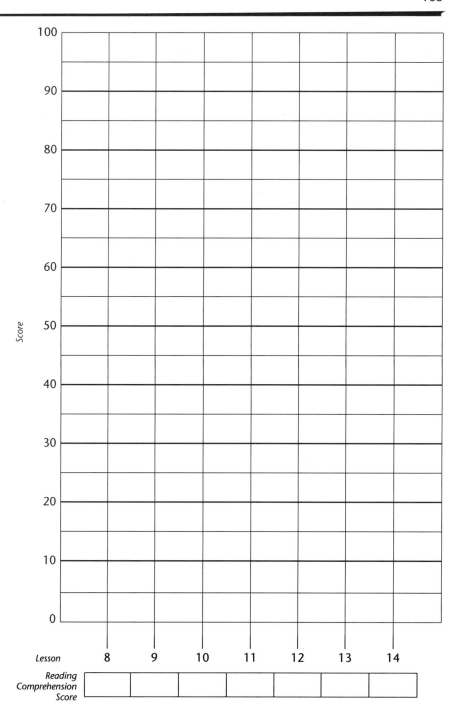

Score

Lesson	8	9	10	11	12	13	14
Reading Comprehension Score							

Plotting Your Progress: Critical Thinking

Unit Two

Directions: Work with your teacher to evaluate your responses to the Critical Thinking questions for each lesson. Then fill in the appropriate spaces in the chart below. For each lesson and each type of Critical Thinking question, do the following: Mark a minus sign (–) in the box to indicate areas in which you feel you could improve. Mark a plus sign (+) to indicate areas in which you feel you did well. Mark a minus-slash-plus sign (–/+) to indicate areas in which you had mixed success. Then write any comments you have about your performance, including ideas for improvement.

Lesson	Author's Approach	Summarizing and Paraphrasing	Critical Thinking
8			
9			
10			
11			
12			
13			
14			

UNIT THREE

NORTON I
Emperor of the United States

Joshua Abraham Norton didn't have a royal bone in his body. He also had no college education, no permanent home, and no money. He wasn't even a citizen of the United States. None of that seemed to bother the 40-year-old Englishman, however, when in 1859 he boldly declared himself emperor of the United States.

2   When Norton moved to the United States in 1849, he had no plans to become emperor. He left England because he had heard about the California gold rush. Gold had been discovered in California, and people were swarming into San Francisco in hopes of striking it rich. Norton figured that he could make money selling scarce goods to the miners. For a while that's just what he did. He set up a shop in downtown San Francisco, in which he sold coffee, tea, flour, and rice. By 1853 he had accumulated a fortune. Then disaster struck. Norton lost all his savings in one bad investment. On top of that, a fire tore through his warehouses, destroying his entire supply of goods. Almost overnight, Joshua Norton found himself bankrupt.

The much-loved eccentric Joshua A. ("Emperor") Norton of San Francisco. In this undated photograph, Emperor Norton is shown in uniform in his traditional pose.

3 The sudden loss of his fortune shattered Norton, making him feel like a total failure. For a while he worked as a clerk for a Chinese rice company. But such low-level work felt humiliating to him after the freedom and power of being on top. So he quit his job, gave up his fancy living quarters, and moved into a cheap little boardinghouse. There he stayed, day after day, alone with his thoughts.

4 Friends who visited him found him tense and depressed at first. The depression faded after a while, but in its place appeared something quite bizarre. Norton began to talk more and more about the political problems of the United States. He saw that the bitter arguments over slavery were leading the country toward civil war. His solution to the problem caught his friends off guard. What the United States needed, Norton began to say, was an emperor. Only an emperor could prevent war and restore peace and harmony to the country. As Norton rambled on, it became clear whom he had in mind for the job.

5 On September 17, 1859, Norton went public with his idea. He walked into the newsroom of the *San Francisco Bulletin* and handed the editor a written notice, asking that it be published in the next edition of the newspaper. At the "request and desire of a large majority of the citizens of these United States," the announcement stated, "I, Joshua Norton,...declare and proclaim myself emperor of these United States...." It was signed "NORTON I, Emperor of the United States."

6 The editor of the *Bulletin* must have found the notice amusing, for he ran it on the front page. There it captured people's attention, and soon everyone in town was talking about the new "emperor." A few days later, Norton made his first public appearance. He dressed in an old blue military uniform, complete with brass buttons and red trim. At his side he wore a heavy sword that he had had custom-made at a blacksmith shop. Then he proudly set out through the streets of San Francisco, greeting everyone he met with a solemn nod.

7 Perhaps people recognized that Norton was basically harmless, or perhaps they sensed how important it was to him to be taken seriously. Maybe they just liked the idea of having their own resident emperor. In any event, they responded to the appearance of Norton I with cheers. The warm welcome convinced Norton that his subjects deserved the very best government they could get. He decided that the members of Congress were too corrupt, so to the amazement of the people of San Francisco, he published a statement dissolving the Congress of the United States. He also announced that he was dissolving the Republic of the United States. No one in Washington, D.C., paid any attention to Norton, but he didn't care. As long as the people in his own city treated him with respect, he was happy.

8 Norton did soon find, however, that running an empire could be quite expensive. After all, an emperor needs shoes, clothes, food, transportation, and lodging. He tried to solve his financial problems by printing his own money. He designed "bonds of the empire," which he declared to be worth 50 cents each. Many shopkeepers found the bonds amusing and agreed to let Norton use them. Still, the

Steamer Day in San Francisco. *This lithograph shows a view of San Francisco in the 1860s.*

bonds did not cover all the royal expenses.

9   To augment his personal funds, Norton devised a system of taxation. He asked each business in the city to pay its fair share of taxes to the empire. He asked small businesses for 25 cents, and larger ones for two or three dollars. Everyone knew that the "taxes" Norton collected went straight into his own pocket, but when he appeared at their doors, all decked out in his royal uniform, few business owners had the heart to turn him down. On a good day Norton took in as much as 25 dollars in taxes.

10   Sometimes Norton asked for more than the usual amount of money. That happened whenever he came up with a grand new vision for promoting world peace. Such visions came to him regularly, and when they did, he would set out in search of financial backing. He would approach a loyal subject of the empire and ask for a loan of hundreds of millions of dollars. Although he never got the loan, he seemed just as happy to get a donation of a dime or two.

11   As emperor of the United States, Norton expected certain privileges. He expected, for example, to eat all his meals for free. He would simply appear at a restaurant, announce his identity, and wait for the management to serve him. Before long, every restaurant owner in San Francisco recognized Norton I. Like everyone else in the city, the restaurant owners found him charming. They always treated him courteously, offered him their best food, and never insulted him by asking him to pay.

12   Norton expected the empire to support him, and in a sense, it did. From 1859 until his death in 1880, a group of old friends paid his rent. Streetcar conductors paid his fares on trolley cars, and his landlord paid his laundry bills. The Central Pacific Railroad issued him a lifetime pass to all its California dining and sleeping cars. And the San Francisco Board of Supervisors voted unanimously to foot the bill for a new set of royal clothes.

13   Despite the way it may sound, Emperor Norton I did not live a carefree life. Many serious problems weighed heavily on his mind. He worried, for example, about the fate of Mexico. He finally decided that Mexico was "entirely unfit to manage her own affairs," so he appointed himself "Protector of Mexico." When the Civil War broke out, Norton felt it was his responsibility to end it. He ordered Abraham Lincoln and Jefferson Davis, the leader of the South, to go to California so he could make peace between them. He could never understand why the two men ignored his command.

14   Norton had many other, smaller duties as well. He felt obligated to wander the city inspecting the streets and water drains. He checked his watch constantly to be sure the streetcars in his empire were running on schedule. He felt he had to attend a different church every Sunday to prevent jealousy among the congregations. And he attended every public meeting to offer his imperial words of wisdom.

15   Sometimes he used the public meetings to seek help on the issues that troubled him most. During one meeting, for instance, he rose and asked the crowd the following question: "Take 25 square miles of land. Let it rain on that land 24 hours. Then turn every one of those drops of water into a baby. How many babies would there be?" He became furious when the bewildered audience could not provide an answer. Finally he just stormed out of the meeting.

16   Incidents such as that one proved to Norton I that his poor lovable subjects simply weren't very bright. That insight made him even more determined to take good care of them.

17   Apparently, the people of San Francisco felt that Norton was a good emperor. When he died after having ruled his empire for 21 years, the entire city went into mourning. His subjects spent $10,000 on his funeral. Eight thousand people filed past his casket. Newspapers wrote loving tributes to him. One newspaper summed up his appeal this way: "The Emperor Norton killed nobody, robbed nobody, and deprived nobody of his country—which is more than can be said for most fellows in his trade." 🍃

If you have been timed while reading this article, enter your reading time below. Then turn to the Words-per-Minute Table on page 195 and look up your reading speed (words per minute). Enter your reading speed on the graph on page 196.

Reading Time: Lesson 15

_____ : _____
Minutes   Seconds

A | Finding the Main Idea

One statement below expresses the main idea of the article. One statement is too general, or too broad. The other statement explains only part of the article; it is too narrow. Label the statements using the following key:

M—Main Idea   **B—Too Broad**   **N—Too Narrow**

_____ 1. For 21 years, Joshua Norton claimed to be emperor of the United States.

_____ 2. As emperor, Joshua Norton worried a great deal about the political problems of the United States and the smooth operation of the city of San Francisco.

_____ 3. Joshua Norton was a charming, harmless eccentric.

_____ Score 15 points for a correct M answer.

_____ Score 5 points for each correct B or N answer.

_____ **Total Score:** Finding the Main Idea

B | Recalling Facts

How well do you remember the facts in the article? Put an X in the box next to the answer that correctly completes each statement about the article.

1. Norton originally emigrated to the United States to
   - ☐ a. make money during the gold rush.
   - ☐ b. declare himself emperor.
   - ☐ c. create a new system of taxation.

2. After losing all his money in 1853, Norton became a
   - ☐ a. bartender in a saloon.
   - ☐ b. clerk for a Chinese rice company.
   - ☐ c. streetcar conductor.

3. Norton proclaimed himself emperor
   - ☐ a. while visiting Washington, D.C.
   - ☐ b. in the _San Francisco Bulletin_.
   - ☐ c. in a letter to the leader of Mexico.

4. Norton planned to end the Civil War by
   - ☐ a. inviting Abraham Lincoln and Jefferson Davis to hold peace talks with him.
   - ☐ b. leading Mexico in an invasion of the United States.
   - ☐ c. having generals from both sides meet in San Francisco for a peace rally.

5. Emperor Norton
   - ☐ a. never went to church.
   - ☐ b. always went to the same church.
   - ☐ c. went to a different church every Sunday.

Score 5 points for each correct answer.

_____ **Total Score:** Recalling Facts

C | Making Inferences

When you combine your own experience and information from a text to draw a conclusion that is not directly stated in that text, you are making an inference. Below are five statements that may or may not be inferences based on information in the article. Label the statements using the following key:

C—Correct Inference   F—Faulty Inference

_____ 1. Most of the people who went to San Francisco during the gold rush were from England.

_____ 2. Norton never came up with a realistic plan for ensuring world peace.

_____ 3. People in Mexico paid no attention to Norton's declaration that he was Protector of Mexico.

_____ 4. Joshua Norton never married.

_____ 5. Small children were afraid of Emperor Norton.

Score 5 points for each correct answer.

_____ **Total Score:** Making Inferences

D | Using Words Precisely

Each numbered sentence below contains an underlined word or phrase from the article. Following the sentence are three definitions. One definition is closest to the meaning of the underlined word. One definition is opposite or nearly opposite. Label those two definitions using the following key. Do not label the remaining definition.

C—Closest   O—Opposite or Nearly Opposite

1. He decided that the members of Congress were too <u>corrupt</u>, so to the amazement of the people of San Francisco, he dissolved the Congress.

_____ a. pure

_____ b. uninformed

_____ c. dishonest

2. To <u>augment</u> his personal funds, Norton devised a system of taxation.

_____ a. add to

_____ b. cut back

_____ c. calculate

3. Such visions came to him regularly, and when they did, he would set out in search of financial <u>backing</u>.

_____ a. information

_____ b. attack

_____ c. support

4. Sometimes he used the public meetings to seek help on the <u>issues</u> that troubled him most.

_____ a. newspapers

_____ b. problems

_____ c. solutions

5. That <u>insight</u> made him even more determined to take good care of them.

_____ a. affection

_____ b. realization

_____ c. oversight

_____ Score 3 points for each correct C answer.

_____ Score 2 points for each correct O answer.

_____ **Total Score:** Using Words Precisely

Enter the four total scores in the spaces below, and add them together to find your Reading Comprehension Score. Then record your score on the graph on page 197.

Score	Question Type	Lesson 15
_____	Finding the Main Idea	
_____	Recalling Facts	
_____	Making Inferences	
_____	Using Words Precisely	
_____	**Reading Comprehension Score**	

Author's Approach

Put an X in the box next to the correct answer.

1. The author uses the first sentence of the article to

☐ a. inform the reader that Joshua Norton was not descended from royalty.

☐ b. describe Norton's bone structure.

☐ c. compare Norton to other emperors.

2. From the statements below, choose the one that you believe the author would agree with.

☐ a. Most of the people of San Francisco considered Norton a nuisance and an embarrassment.

☐ b. Norton had a great deal of influence on the federal government.

☐ c. Norton really believed that he was emperor of the United States.

3. What does the author imply by saying "Norton did soon find, however, that running an empire could be quite expensive"?

☐ a. Norton considered stepping down as emperor because his expenses were so high.

☐ b. Norton discovered that ruling the United States cost more than he had thought it would.

☐ c. Norton needed money for his own living expenses.

4. Choose the statement below that best describes the author's position in paragraph 13.

☐ a. Many of the world's leaders depended on Emperor Norton to help them solve their problems.

☐ b. Although Emperor Norton believed that he had an important role to play in world affairs, no one took him seriously.

☐ c. It was Emperor Norton's responsibility to end the Civil War.

_____ Number of correct answers

Record your personal assessment of your work on the Critical Thinking Chart on page 198.

Summarizing and Paraphrasing

Follow the directions provided for question 1. Put an X in the box next to the correct answer for the other questions.

1. Complete the following one-sentence summary of the article using the lettered phrases from the phrase bank below. Write the letters on the lines.

Phrase Bank:
a. his proclamation of himself as emperor
b. his subjects' grief over his death
c. his actions as emperor and his relationship with his subjects

The article about Emperor Norton begins with _____, goes on to explain _____, and ends with _____.

2. Below are summaries of the article. Choose the summary that says all the most important things about the article but in the fewest words.

☐ a. After Joshua Norton became emperor of the United States, he printed his own money and asked businesses in San Francisco to pay taxes to the empire. Although Norton tried to solve serious world problems, no one really listened to him.

☐ b. Joshua Norton proclaimed himself emperor of the United States, but he failed to put an end to the Civil War.

☐ c. After Joshua Norton declared himself emperor of the United States, the people of San Francisco humored him. They took care of his expenses, fed him, and truly mourned him when he died.

3. Choose the best one-sentence paraphrase for the following sentence from the article:

"Perhaps people recognized that Norton was basically harmless, or perhaps they sensed how important it was to him to be taken seriously."

☐ a. Maybe people knew who Norton was, or perhaps they really took him seriously.

☐ b. It might have been that people realized that Norton was not dangerous in any way, or maybe they recognized how much he longed for respect.

☐ c. Maybe some people realized that Norton wasn't going to hurt them, or they sensed that he would become an important person.

_____ Number of correct answers

Record your personal assessment of your work on the Critical Thinking Chart on page 198.

CRITICAL THINKING

Critical Thinking

Put an X in the box next to the correct answer for questions 1, 2, and 4. Follow the directions provided for the other question.

1. Which of the following statements from the article is an opinion rather than a fact?

☐ a. Only an emperor could prevent war and restore peace and harmony to the country.

☐ b. Norton lost all his savings in one bad investment.

☐ c. From 1859 until his death in 1880, a group of old friends paid his rent.

2. From what the article told about the people of San Francisco, you can conclude that they

☐ a. were relieved by Emperor Norton's death.

☐ b. probably insisted on electing the next emperor.

☐ c. would be likely to appreciate other harmless eccentrics.

3. Choose from the letters below to correctly complete the following statement. Write the letters on the lines.

In the article, _____ and _____ are alike because they both contributed to Norton's expenses.

a. San Francisco streetcar conductors
b. the Congress of the United States
c. officials of the Central Pacific Railroad

4. What did you have to do to answer question 2?

☐ a. find an opinion (what someone thinks about something)

☐ b. find a comparison (how things are the same)

☐ c. draw a conclusion (a sensible statement based on the text and your experience)

_____ Number of correct answers

Record your personal assessment of your work on the Critical Thinking Chart on page 198.

Personal Response

I wonder why

_____

_____

_____

_____

Self-Assessment

While reading the article, I found it easiest to

_____

_____

_____

_____

CARRY NATION
Fighting the "Hellish Poison"

A saloon in New York's Bowery district in 1905. Places such as this were the target of Carry Nation's wrath and hatchet.

Mr. Dobson didn't know what hit him. On June 6, 1900, Carry Amelia Nation stormed into his saloon in Kiowa, Kansas. In a clear, calm voice, Carry told the customers, "I have come to save you from a drunkard's fate." She then proceeded to destroy the place.

2   Although she was 54 years old at the time, Carry was still a ruggedly built woman. Nearly six feet tall, she weighed 175 pounds and had extremely muscular arms. As the patrons watched in stunned silence, Carry set her imposing strength loose on poor Mr. Dobson's saloon. Heaving brick after brick, she smashed every mirror, glass, and bottle in the place. Then she slapped her hands together and looked the shocked proprietor straight in the eye. "Now, Mr. Dobson," she said, "I have finished. God be with you."

3   Carry had nothing personal against Mr. Dobson. She just hated liquor and the establishments that served that "hellish poison." Carry's first husband, Dr. Charles Gloyd, had been addicted to whiskey and had drunk himself to death in 1869, after only two years of marriage. That set Carry

on the road to becoming an outspoken advocate of prohibition. Prohibition is the forbidding by law of the manufacture and sale of alcoholic beverages.

4 In 1877 Carry married David Nation, a journalist, lawyer, and minister. Her religious beliefs grew stricter and stronger, and she took her new name, Carry A. Nation, as a sign that she was destined to help improve the moral welfare of the country. In 1890 she began to speak against the evils of liquor and to pray outside saloons. She soon combined her prayers with action.

5 On June 5, 1900, Carry had a dream in which a voice commanded her: "Take something in your hands and throw it at those places and smash them!" That was all Carry needed to hear. The next morning she picked up several dozen bricks, hitched up her horse to her buggy, and drove straight to Mr. Dobson's saloon.

6 After trashing that bar, she got back into her buggy and started to drive away, when suddenly a wonderful idea popped into her head. She still had a lot of bricks left, so with a gleam in her eye, she hurled two of them through Mr. Dobson's front windows. Then she went on to demolish two more saloons in Kiowa before finally running out of ammunition. Because she wanted to draw public attention to her campaign, she made no effort to leave town, and even demanded that the sheriff arrest her. The bewildered sheriff refused to do that. Carry had caught the town so off-guard that no one knew quite what to make of her or what to do with her.

7 The confusion was understandable. After all, under Kansas law, liquor and the saloons that served it were illegal. The police, however, generally ignored the law, and saloons flourished in every city and town in the state. Carry Nation had written letters of protest to the governor and to all the local newspapers, but nothing had come of her efforts. Finally, since the saloons were illegal, Carry decided that she was perfectly within her rights in destroying them.

8 Flushed with success, Carry extended her rampage to include every saloon in Kansas. She headed off to Wichita, the liquor capital of the state, where wholesale liquor warehouses and saloons abounded. Since she considered saloon-smashing a serious and honorable business, she dressed for the occasion. She wore a black dress with pearl buttons, square-toed shoes, and a black bonnet with a silk ribbon tied under her chin.

9 After surveying all the saloons in Wichita, Carry decided to start by taking on the most elegant one of all. It was situated in the basement of the Hotel Carey. Carry walked into the saloon and threw a brick through the huge mirror that hung over the bar. Then, with relentless determination, she destroyed the pictures of partially clothed women that decorated the walls. Finally, she took out a foot-long iron bar and smashed all the bottles and glasses behind the bar. Just as the last bottle hit the floor, the police arrived.

Carry Nation, in full-battle pose, ready to take on the evils of drink

10   "Madam," declared one officer, "I must arrest you for defacing property."

11   "Defacing?" she cried. "Defacing? I am defacing nothing! I am *destroying*."

12   After a short stay in the local jail, Carry was released. By that time she had become the most notorious woman in the United States. Many people condemned her as a nut, but there were a considerable number who shared her hatred of alcohol. Every day Carry received hundreds of letters and telegrams congratulating her on her noble work. That, of course, only encouraged her to seek out new saloons to wreck. After her jail stint, she began using a distinctive new weapon: a hatchet. Carry used it not only to break mirrors and bottles, but also to hack at the wooden bars—the counters—themselves.

13   Carry Nation raided dozens of saloons in Kansas and neighboring states. Sometimes she was accompanied by women who sang hymns as she smashed. Other times she worked alone, singing, praying, and shouting passages from the Bible at the patrons of the bar. Smart saloon owners either closed their doors when Carry was in the neighborhood or hired armed guards to keep her outside. Still, she made many successful raids.

14   The police arrested her over 30 times, usually on the grounds of "disturbing the peace." Often the judge would fine her for damages or ask her to leave town. To raise money to pay her numerous fines, Carry gave speeches and sold souvenir autographed hatchets. She railed not only against liquor but also against tobacco, corsets, and "improper" dress for women (short skirts), all of which she considered evils of society. Her work inspired other "hatchet women" to attack the bars in their neighborhoods.

15   Gradually, though, the excitement Carry stirred up began to die down. People grew tired of her unique brand of lawlessness. Many peaceful members of anti-liquor groups wanted nothing to do with her. Carry tried to rekindle the fires of moral outrage by giving lectures in the United States and Europe. But more often than not the audience would greet her with hoots and showers of rotten vegetables rather than with applause.

16   Still, Carry continued to strike saloons from time to time. In 1909 she attacked a barroom in Washington's Union Depot with three hatchets she called Faith, Hope, and Charity. In January 1910, in Butte, Montana, she hit her last saloon. In that bar Carry Nation met her match: a powerful young woman named May Maloy. When Carry tried to force her way into May's saloon, May gave her a sound beating. After that, Carry retired her hatchets, and the saloonkeepers of the Midwest breathed a long sigh of relief. 🍂

If you have been timed while reading this article, enter your reading time below. Then turn to the Words-per-Minute Table on page 195 and look up your reading speed (words per minute). Enter your reading speed on the graph on page 196.

Reading Time: Lesson 16

_____ : _____
Minutes   *Seconds*

A Finding the Main Idea

One statement below expresses the main idea of the article. One statement is too general, or too broad. The other statement explains only part of the article; it is too narrow. Label the statements using the following key:

M—Main Idea   **B—Too Broad**   **N—Too Narrow**

_____ 1. Carry Nation fought the sale of liquor by wrecking saloons.

_____ 2. Carry Nation used violence in her campaign against drinking.

_____ 3. Carry Nation often used a hatched to smash saloons.

_____ Score 15 points for a correct M answer.

_____ Score 5 points for each correct B or N answer.

_____ **Total Score:** Finding the Main Idea

B Recalling Facts

How well do you remember the facts in the article? Put an X in the box next to the answer that correctly completes each statement about the article.

1. Carry did most of her saloon-smashing in
☐ a. Kansas.
☐ b. Washington.
☐ c. New York.

2. Carry's first husband was
☐ a. the sheriff of Wichita.
☐ b. addicted to whiskey.
☐ c. killed by a bartender.

3. Carry came up with an idea of saloon-smashing after hearing
☐ a. a speech by the editor of her local newspaper.
☐ b. her husband preach against alcohol.
☐ c. a voice in a dream.

4. The police
☐ a. never arrested Carry.
☐ b. arrested Carry over 30 times.
☐ c. often beat Carry.

5. Faith, Hope, and Charity were the names Carry gave to three
☐ a. saloons she destroyed.
☐ b. hatchets.
☐ c. governors who supported her efforts.

Score 5 points for each correct answer.

_____ **Total Score:** Recalling Facts

C | Making Inferences

When you combine your own experience and information from a text to draw a conclusion that is not directly stated in that text, you are making an inference. Below are five statements that may or may not be inferences based on information in the article. Label the statements using the following key:

C—Correct Inference   F—Faulty Inference

_____ 1. Her second husband, David Nation, enthusiastically supported and aided Carry in her anti-liquor campaign.

_____ 2. When Carry Nation was on her rampage, Kansas was the only state in the country that had laws prohibiting the sale of alcohol.

_____ 3. The Hotel Carey was an elegant place.

_____ 4. Carry did not want anyone to know that it was she who was smashing saloons.

_____ 5. Most saloonkeepers were afraid of Carry Nation.

Score 5 points for each correct answer.

_____ **Total Score:** Making Inferences

D | Using Words Precisely

Each numbered sentence below contains an underlined word or phrase from the article. Following the sentence are three definitions. One definition is closest to the meaning of the underlined word. One definition is opposite or nearly opposite. Label those two definitions using the following key. Do not label the remaining definition.

C—Closest   O—Opposite or Nearly Opposite

1. As the patrons watched in stunned silence, Carry set her <u>imposing</u> strength loose on poor Mr. Dobson's saloon.

_____ a. ordinary

_____ b. impressive

_____ c. religious

2. That set Carry on the road to becoming an outspoken <u>advocate</u> of prohibition.

_____ a. opponent

_____ b. promoter

_____ c. lawyer

3. She headed off to Wichita, the liquor capital of the state, where wholesale liquor warehouses and saloons <u>abounded</u>.

_____ a. were illegal

_____ b. were scarce

_____ c. were plentiful

4. By that time she had become the most <u>notorious</u> woman in the United States.

_____ a. unfavorably famous

_____ b. hated

_____ c. little known

5. Carry tried to <u>rekindle</u> the fires of moral outrage by giving lectures in the United States and Europe.

_____ a. watch over

_____ b. put an end to

_____ c. stir up again

_____ Score 3 points for each correct C answer.

_____ Score 2 points for each correct O answer.

_____ **Total Score:** Using Words Precisely

Enter the four total scores in the spaces below, and add them together to find your Reading Comprehension Score. Then record your score on the graph on page 197.

Score	Question Type	Lesson 16
_____	Finding the Main Idea	
_____	Recalling Facts	
_____	Making Inferences	
_____	Using Words Precisely	
_____	**Reading Comprehension Score**	

Author's Approach

Put an X in the box next to the correct answer.

1. What does the author mean by the statement "After that, Carry retired her hatchets, and the saloonkeepers of the Midwest breathed a long sigh of relief"?

☐ a. Midwestern saloonkeepers had difficulty breathing after Carry retired.

☐ b. When Carry's hatchets broke, Midwestern saloonkeepers held their breath.

☐ c. Midwestern saloonkeepers were greatly relieved after Carry Nation stopped wrecking saloons.

2. Which of the following statements from the article best describes Carry Nation's thoughts and opinions?

☐ a. "Nearly six feet tall, she weighed 175 pounds and had extremely muscular arms."

☐ b. "She just hated liquor and the establishments that served that 'hellish poison.'"

☐ c. "She wore a black dress with pearl buttons, square-toed shoes, and a black bonnet with a silk ribbon tied under her chin."

3. How is the author's purpose for writing the article expressed in paragraph 5?

☐ a. The author suggests that Carry had an active imagination.

☐ b. The author explains what led Carry to begin smashing saloons.

☐ c. The author expresses an opinion supporting Carry's decision to smash saloons.

4. The author probably wrote this article in order to

☐ a. tell the reader about Carry Nation and her efforts to halt the sale of liquor.

☐ b. inform the reader about the dangers of drinking alcohol.

☐ c. persuade the reader to take a stand for or against prohibition.

_____ Number of correct answers

Record your personal assessment of your work on the Critical Thinking Chart on page 198.

Summarizing and Paraphrasing

Follow the directions provided for question 1. Put an X in the box next to the correct answer for question 2.

1. Look for the important ideas and events in paragraphs 3 and 4. Summarize those paragraphs in one or two sentences.

_____

_____

_____

2. Read the statement about the article below. Then read the paraphrase of that statement. Choose the reason that best tells why the paraphrase does not say the same thing as the statement.

Statement: Carry Nation spoke out against the evils of alcohol and demolished saloons in Kansas because she felt that it was her duty to help improve the moral welfare of the country.

Paraphrase: Carry Nation felt that it was her duty to support prohibition.

☐ a. Paraphrase says too much.

☐ b. Paraphrase doesn't say enough.

☐ c. Paraphrase doesn't agree with the statement about the article.

_____ Number of correct answers

Record your personal assessment of your work on the Critical Thinking Chart on page 198.

Critical Thinking

Put an X in the box next to the correct answer for questions 1, 3, and 4. Follow the directions provided for the other questions.

1. Judging by Carry Nation's actions as described in this article, you can predict that she would have

☐ a. supported the 18th amendment ratified in 1919 which forbade the manufacture, sale, and transportation of alcohol.

☐ b. supported the repeal of Prohibition in 1933.

☐ c. trusted the authorities to enforce the 18th amendment without help from her.

CRITICAL THINKING

2. Choose from the letters below to correctly complete the following statement. Write the letters on the lines.

In the article, _____ and _____ are different.

a. the reaction of the barkeeper at the Hotel Carey to Carry's actions

b. the reaction of Mr. Dobson to Carry's actions

c. the reaction of May Maloy to Carry's actions

3. What was the cause of Carry's becoming an outspoken advocate of prohibition?

☐ a. She prayed against the evils of liquor outside of saloons.

☐ b. Her second husband, David Nation, drank himself to death.

☐ c. Her first husband, Dr. Charles Gloyd, drank himself to death.

4. How is Carry Nation an example of an eccentric?

☐ a. She engaged in outrageous behavior to fight for what she believed was right.

☐ b. Whenever she went saloon-smashing, she dressed up for the occasion.

☐ c. She remarried after her first husband died.

5. In which paragraph did you find your information or details to answer question 3?

_____

_____ Number of correct answers

Record your personal assessment of your work on the Critical Thinking Chart on page 198.

Personal Response

How do you think you would feel if someone like Carry Nation began destroying movie theaters because she felt they were evil?

_____

_____

_____

_____

Self-Assessment

When reading the article, I was having trouble with

_____

_____

_____

_____

CRITICAL THINKING

VINCENT VAN GOGH
Tragic Genius

Vincent van Gogh in a self-portrait painted in 1887

My stomach has become terribly weak," wrote Vincent van Gogh in 1877. It was no wonder. The 24-year-old Dutchman lived mostly on bread and coffee. He slept little, smoked a lot, and wandered the dark streets of Amsterdam, in the Netherlands, hour after hour.

2 Although van Gogh was only a young man at the time, he had already failed at three different careers. First he had tried to be an art dealer in England, an occupation selected for him by his father and uncle. But van Gogh did not have the temperament to serve the public; he argued too much with the customers. His prickly manner grew more pronounced after he was rejected by a young woman he adored. It didn't take long for the owner of the art gallery to fire him.

3 Next van Gogh had attempted to be a preacher, a position his father had held for many years. After yet another failure, van Gogh had tried his hand as a bookseller. He didn't last long at that, either. With grim determination, van Gogh then moved to Amsterdam to search for a new direction for his life.

4 The letters he wrote to his brother Theo indicate how difficult van Gogh

found life at that time. "My head is sometimes heavy," he wrote from Amsterdam, "and often it burns and my thoughts are confused." He viewed the world in a way that nobody else seemed to understand. He wanted companionship, yet he alienated almost all of his acquaintances with his quarrelsome attitude. He wanted to be successful at something, yet he couldn't find employment he liked. Still, he had moments of hope. One day he confided to Theo, "My conscience tells me there is something greater in my future."

5   It took van Gogh three more years to figure out what that "something greater" was. For a while he believed the answer was to live among the poor, nursing the sick and comforting the friendless. With that in mind, he became a missionary in Belgium. But van Gogh alarmed his fellow missionaries; he was a little too enthusiastic for their tastes. They were shocked when he gave away most of his belongings and began spending his nights in a hovel. Word soon went out to van Gogh that his services as a missionary were no longer needed.

6   In March 1880, van Gogh decided to visit the studio of Jules Breton, an artist he admired. Despite the fact that it was a 30-mile trip, van Gogh chose to walk. For three days and three nights, he trudged along, sleeping out in the open and asking for crusts of bread along the way. When he reached his destination, he was too intimidated to introduce himself to Breton. He stood outside the man's studio, racked with fear, then simply turned and walked home.

7   The trip wasn't a total waste of time, however, for during that journey van Gogh made up his mind once and for all to be a painter. He believed painting was a noble choice since it would allow him to remain poor—an important consideration for a man who thought money corrupted men's souls. "I consciously choose the dog's path through life," he announced to his brother. "I shall be poor; I shall be a painter; I want to remain human."

8   Van Gogh dedicated himself entirely to painting. He moved to France and began studying the works of other artists. He also took art classes, but van Gogh's teachers were scornful of his work. They complained that he did not follow their instructions but instead pursued his own odd ideas. One instructor called his paintings "putrefied dogs."

9   Despite his instructors' criticisms, van Gogh kept working. He experimented with lines, color, texture, and shading. For a while, he allied himself with the Impressionists, a group of artists who tried to bring their canvases to life by using dabs of unmixed colors. Soon, however, van Gogh broke out on his own. In art, as in life, he wasn't content to follow other people's rules.

10   One of van Gogh's innovations involved a way to capture night scenes.

One of van Gogh's most famous paintings, Sunflowers, sold for $40.3 million in 1987. Recently there has been some question as to whether it is a genuine van Gogh or a fake.

He wanted to paint people enjoying an evening at an outdoor café, but he didn't want to draw the scene from memory. He wanted to sketch it as it unfolded. To capture the scene properly, he went out into the night with candles stuck on the brim of his hat. In the candlelight that flickered around his head, he painted *Café Terrace at Night.*

11   Throughout the 1880s, van Gogh developed his artistic genius. He sold very few paintings, but his brother Theo sent him money for paints and other necessities. Using his meager supplies, van Gogh produced tender paintings of mothers with children. He painted sunflowers and irises bursting with color. He painted quiet villages and stormy wheat fields. Although these paintings were generally ignored during van Gogh's lifetime, they are highly valued by art lovers today. Many are worth millions of dollars.

12   Sometimes van Gogh was pleased with his efforts. More often, though, he despaired of ever producing anything of value. "It is absolutely certain that I shall never do important things," he wrote at one low point.

13   Van Gogh's unhappiness revealed itself in many ways. His self-portraits disclosed the mad swirling of his thoughts. His letters to Theo expressed loneliness and discontent. "How I'd like to settle down and have a home!" he wrote in one note.

"Often whole days pass without my speaking to anyone," he lamented in another.

14   Although van Gogh expressed the desire for human intimacy, his actions didn't reflect that longing. He worked in solitude with a strange fervor, often going extended periods without eating or sleeping. To make matters worse, he drank heavily. And in December 1888, he did something so bizarre and grotesque that people today still shudder at the thought of it.

15   On Christmas Eve, while drinking in a tavern, van Gogh and one of his few friends quarreled. The friend stormed off, and van Gogh retreated to his rented room. There he took a razor and cut off his own right ear. Holding it in his hand, he went to the home of a woman he knew only slightly. He handed the bloody ear to her, saying, "Keep this object like a treasure." Then he went back to his room and passed out from loss of blood.

16   Soon after that incident, van Gogh ended up in a hospital for the mentally disturbed. He spent most of the next year in a room with barred windows. During that time, he had moments of lucidity when he produced beautiful paintings. He also had dark moments when he ate his own paints or sat, staring, unable to do anything.

17   In the spring of 1890, van Gogh left the hospital and moved to the small French town of Auvers-Sur-Oise. There he painted 70 canvases in 70 days. It was an unbelievable burst of creativity. But it did not signal an inner peace. Rather, it was a precursor to van Gogh's final desperate act. On the afternoon of July 27, 1890, van Gogh went out to the field where he had been painting earlier in the day. He pulled out a revolver and shot himself in the chest. After he staggered back to his room, his horrified neighbors summoned his brother Theo. Two days later, Vincent van Gogh died from his wound. ✒

If you have been timed while reading this article, enter your reading time below. Then turn to the Words-per-Minute Table on page 195 and look up your reading speed (words per minute). Enter your reading speed on the graph on page 196.

Reading Time: Lesson 17

_____ : _____

Minutes   Seconds

A | Finding the Main Idea

One statement below expresses the main idea of the article. One statement is too general, or too broad. The other statement explains only part of the article; it is too narrow. Label the statements using the following key:

M—Main Idea   **B—Too Broad**   **N—Too Narrow**

_____ 1. Vincent van Gogh was a man with great talents and great problems.

_____ 2. After an argument, Vincent van Gogh cut off his ear and gave it to a woman he knew only slightly.

_____ 3. Painter Vincent van Gogh was an artistic genius who often questioned his own talent and sometimes suffered episodes of unusual, even destructive, behavior.

_____ Score 15 points for a correct M answer.

_____ Score 5 points for each correct B or N answer.

_____ **Total Score:** Finding the Main Idea

B | Recalling Facts

How well do you remember the facts in the article? Put an X in the box next to the answer that correctly completes each statement about the article.

1. After van Gogh failed at three different careers, he moved to
   - ☐ a. England.
   - ☐ b. Belgium.
   - ☐ c. Amsterdam.

2. After walking 30 miles to the studio of artist Jules Breton, van Gogh
   - ☐ a. turned back and walked home.
   - ☐ b. introduced himself to Breton.
   - ☐ c. became a missionary.

3. Van Gogh's teachers in France
   - ☐ a. admired his work.
   - ☐ b. imitated his work.
   - ☐ c. disliked his work.

4. After he cut off his ear, van Gogh spent most of the next year in
   - ☐ a. the small French town of Auvers-Sur-Oise.
   - ☐ b. a hospital for the mentally disturbed.
   - ☐ c. his brother Theo's home.

5. On July 27, 1890, van Gogh
   - ☐ a. cut off his brother Theo's right ear.
   - ☐ b. shot himself in the chest.
   - ☐ c. cut off his own right ear.

Score 5 points for each correct answer.

_____ **Total Score:** Recalling Facts

C Making Inferences

When you combine your own experience and information from a text to draw a conclusion that is not directly stated in that text, you are making an inference. Below are five statements that may or may not be inferences based on information in the article. Label the statements using the following key:

C—Correct Inference   **F—Faulty Inference**

_____ 1. Vincent van Gogh was unwilling to work hard.

_____ 2. Theo saved many of the letters that Vincent sent him.

_____ 3. Artists in van Gogh's day did not expect to make much money.

_____ 4. Van Gogh's instructors were unable recognize the artist's genius only because his talents were not fully developed at the time he studied with them.

_____ 5. One reason van Gogh had to stay in a mental hospital is because he posed a threat to his own life.

Score 5 points for each correct answer.

_____ **Total Score:** Making Inferences

D Using Words Precisely

Each numbered sentence below contains an underlined word or phrase from the article. Following the sentence are three definitions. One definition is closest to the meaning of the underlined word. One definition is opposite or nearly opposite. Label those two definitions using the following key. Do not label the remaining definition.

C—Closest   O—Opposite or Nearly Opposite

1. His <u>prickly</u> manner grew more pronounced after he was rejected by a young woman he adored.

   _____ a. dryly humorous

   _____ b. bad-tempered

   _____ c. easy-going

2. He wanted companionship, yet he alienated almost all of his acquaintances with his <u>quarrelsome</u> attitude.

   _____ a. agreeable

   _____ b. self-doubting

   _____ c. argumentative

3. Van Gogh's teachers were <u>scornful</u> of his work.

   _____ a. contemptuous

   _____ b. full of admiration

   _____ c. frightened

4. Van Gogh used his <u>meager</u> supplies to produce tender paintings of mothers with children.

   _____ a. abundant

   _____ b. painting

   _____ c. insufficient

5. During that time, he had moments of <u>lucidity</u> when he produced beautiful paintings.

_____ a. mental confusion

_____ b. clearness of thought

_____ c. self-confidence

_____ Score 3 points for each correct C answer.

_____ Score 2 points for each correct O answer.

_____ **Total Score:** Using Words Precisely

Enter the four total scores in the spaces below, and add them together to find your Reading Comprehension Score. Then record your score on the graph on page 197.

Score	Question Type	Lesson 17
_____	Finding the Main Idea	
_____	Recalling Facts	
_____	Making Inferences	
_____	Using Words Precisely	
_____	**Reading Comprehension Score**	

Author's Approach

Put an X in the box next to the correct answer.

1. What does the author mean by the statement "In art, as in life, he wasn't content to follow other people's rules"?

☐ a. Van Gogh lived his life and expressed himself artistically without caring much about what other people thought.

☐ b. Van Gogh wasn't happy because he disagreed with other people's rules.

☐ c. Van Gogh had trouble getting along in society because he was constantly breaking the law.

2. What is the author's purpose in writing "Vincent van Gogh: Tragic Genius"?

☐ a. To encourage readers to pursue their interests at any cost

☐ b. To express an opinion about the lives of artists

☐ c. To describe van Gogh's artistry and personality

3. How is the author's purpose for writing the article expressed in paragraph 10?

☐ a. The author expresses an opinion about van Gogh's painting *Café Terrace at Night*.

☐ b. The author tells about the method van Gogh invented to capture night scenes.

☐ c. The author encourages the reader to learn from van Gogh's creativity.

4. The author tells this story mainly by

☐ a. retelling some of van Gogh's personal experiences.

☐ b. comparing different artists.

☐ c. using his or her imagination and creativity to tell van Gogh's story.

_____ Number of correct answers

Record your personal assessment of your work on the Critical Thinking Chart on page 198.

Summarizing and Paraphrasing

Put an X in the box next to the correct answer.

1. Below are summaries of the article. Choose the summary that says all the most important things about the article but in the fewest words.

☐ a. After Vincent van Gogh chose to take up painting, he discovered his true talent.

☐ b. Vincent van Gogh worked hard to develop his artistic genius, although few others recognized his talent during his lifetime.

☐ c. After failing to achieve success in several different careers, Vincent van Gogh became an inventive, creative artist. Eventually, however, his self-doubt as an artist and unhappiness with his personal life drove him to commit suicide.

CRITICAL THINKING

2. Choose the best one-sentence paraphrase for the following sentence from the article:

"He believed painting was a noble choice since it would allow him to remain poor—an important consideration for a man who thought money corrupted men's souls."

☐ a. Van Gogh believed that being a poor painter was an admirable career because he feared the effect money often has on people.

☐ b. Van Gogh thought that all poor people, but especially artists, were noble because they had no money.

☐ c. Van Gogh wanted to remain poor because he had no use for money.

_____ Number of correct answers

Record your personal assessment of your work on the Critical Thinking Chart on page 198.

Critical Thinking

Put an X in the box next to the correct answer for questions 1, 3, and 4. Follow the directions provided for the other questions.

1. Judging by what the article told about Theo, you can predict that he

☐ a. did not care much about the death of his brother.

☐ b. was saddened by his brother's death.

☐ c. became a painter after his brother's death.

2. Choose from the letters below to correctly complete the following statement. Write the letters on the lines.

On the positive side, _____, but on the negative side _____.

a. Van Gogh longed for human intimacy without achieving it

b. Van Gogh studied the works of other artists in France

c. Van Gogh created masterpieces that are highly valued today

3. What was the cause of van Gogh's fainting spell in December 1888?

☐ a. He had lost a lot of blood after cutting off his ear.

☐ b. He had been quarreling with a friend.

☐ c. He gave his bloody ear to a woman he knew only slightly.

4. How is Vincent van Gogh an example of an eccentric?

☐ a. He was an artist.

☐ b. He made and lived by his own rules.

☐ c. He remained poor throughout his life.

5. In which paragraph did you find your information or details to answer question 3?

_____

_____ Number of correct answers

Record your personal assessment of your work on the Critical Thinking Chart on page 198.

Personal Response

I wonder why

_____

_____

_____

_____

Self-Assessment

From reading this article, I have learned

_____

_____

_____

CRITICAL THINKING

AMANDA FEILDING
Woman with a Hole in Her Head

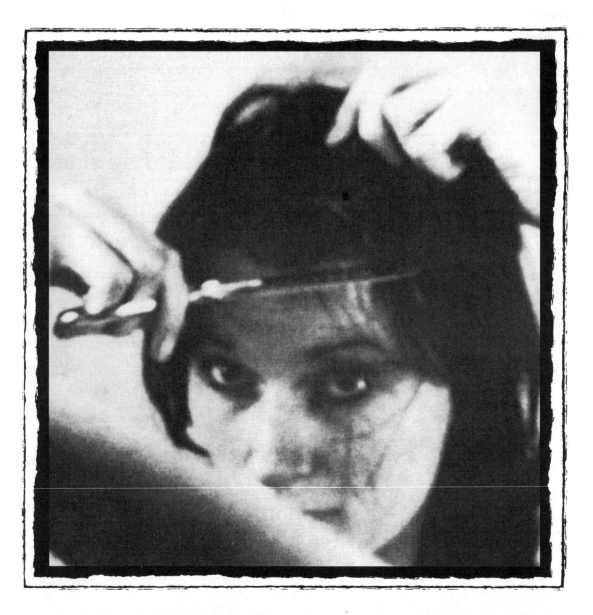

Amanda Feilding is a thin, dark-haired English woman who looks perfectly normal—until you spot the hole in her head. Feilding doesn't mind having people stare at it. She isn't embarrassed or ashamed. In fact, she's proud of the hole. She thinks the world would be a happier place if more people drilled holes through their skulls.

2   Feilding is not the first person to subscribe to this belief. Trepanation, or the process of cutting an opening in the skull and removing part of the bone, is a practice that has been around for centuries. Sometimes trepanning is done for medical reasons—usually to relieve pressure on the brain after a skull fracture. But at other times, it is performed for spiritual or magical purposes. In the Kissii tribe of western Kenya, for instance, trepanning is thought to cure headaches and mental illness.

3   The ancient Romans knew about trepanning. A Roman scholar named Aulus Celsus wrote detailed descriptions of the procedure around A.D. 40. The ancient people of Latin America also practiced trepanation. More than ten thousand trepanned skulls have been

Amanda Feilding cuts her hair in preparation for boring her skull with an electric drill.

unearthed in Peru alone. Scientists have checked on the recovery rate of these Peruvian patients. Judging from signs of healing, about 62 percent survived the operation. Since there was no anesthesia in those days, we can only wonder who was luckier: those who lived through the procedure, or those who died before the pain became too intense.

4   The earliest evidence of trepanation comes from a 7,000-year-old skeleton found in France. This man actually had two holes cut in his head. Close examination shows that he was about 50 years old when he died. He had suffered no disease or injury that would have led to trepanation. Still, he had a big hole in the front of his head. A piece of skull more than two inches in diameter had been removed. The skin over the hole had healed by the time of his death. A second hole, this one more than three inches wide, had partially healed. No one knows what killed this man. But he did not die from the trepanation procedure.

5   It is not clear whether Amanda Feilding knows the long history of trepanation. But it wasn't tales from ancient times that inspired her. It was the words of a friend named Dr. Bart Huges.

6   In 1962, Huges made what he considered to be an important discovery.

He found that a person's consciousness is directly tied to the volume of blood in the brain. If there isn't enough blood getting through, a person becomes faint and weak. He or she may even lose consciousness altogether. So increasing the flow of blood, Dr. Huges reasoned, would increase a person's consciousness. It would make the person more alert, more insightful.

7   However, Huges realized that there was a limit to the amount of blood that could get to the brain. That's because the human skull encases the adult brain. The heart pumps plenty of blood to the cranium, but only so much can fit inside the skull at any particular moment.

A surgeon trephines the skull of a patient.

8　This limitation irritated Dr. Huges, and he searched for a way around it. Then a thought occurred to him: babies' brains aren't enclosed by their skulls. They have a soft spot on the top of their head. This soft spot disappears later, when the skull grows together.

9　Huges believed that babies have a higher form of consciousness than adults. They have more vivid imaginations and a keener ability to perceive things. They aren't caught up in fears, worries, and superstitions.

10　Reasoning from these "facts," Huges concluded that adults could return to their original level of awareness by reopening their soft spots. To do that, they simply had to cut holes in their heads.

11　Although Huges professed confidence in his ideas, he didn't actually try trepanation himself. Instead, he convinced Amanda Feilding and her boyfriend, Joey Mellen, to do it. Mellen tried the procedure first. Using a tool that resembled a corkscrew, he attempted to saw through his skull. Very soon, he discovered that he couldn't do it alone; his skull bone was too hard. Later, Feilding agreed to act as his assistant. As she helped him drill into the bone, Mellen fainted. Feilding called an ambulance, and Mellen ended up in the hospital, where doctors warned him never to try such a stunt again.

12　But still Mellen persisted. In 1970, using an electric drill, he managed to put a sizable hole in his head. Amazingly, he lived to tell about it. In fact, Mellen wrote a book called *Bore Hole* that told all about his experiences. In it, he claims that trepanation has given him more inner peace than he had ever known before. He believes he has attained a spiritual freedom that few other people have achieved.

13　Meanwhile, Amanda Feilding decided it was her turn. She wanted to join Mellen on his higher plane of consciousness. Feilding hoped others would follow her, but she understood that most people would be frightened. To ease their anxieties, she arranged to have Mellen film her as she trepanned herself. She believed the video would be reassuring to potential trepanners.

14　With the camera rolling, Feilding shaved a portion of her head. She used a scalpel to cut through her skin. Then she picked up an electric drill and didn't stop drilling until blood came gushing from her head. Then she set down her instruments and looked toward the camera, smiling broadly.

15　Later, Feilding added a soundtrack of soothing music to the video, which she titled *Heartbeat in the Brain*. Feilding carries the video with her when she travels around England. In various lecture halls and auditoriums, she recounts the many benefits of trepanation. She shows the film to anyone willing to watch it. But even the hardiest viewers have trouble sitting through it. Many people pass out when the blood starts to fly.

16　Feilding has tried other ways to encourage people to put holes in their heads. Twice she has run for a seat in Parliament, campaigning on the platform that the government should pay for people to get trepanned. Not surprisingly, she hasn't captured many votes.

17　Perhaps Feilding will run for public office again someday. If she does, she might consider this slogan: "You need Amanda Feilding in Parliament like you need a hole in the head." 🌿

If you have been timed while reading this article, enter your reading time below. Then turn to the Words-per-Minute Table on page 195 and look up your reading speed (words per minute). Enter your reading speed on the graph on page 196.

Reading Time: Lesson 18

_____ : _____
Minutes　　*Seconds*

A | Finding the Main Idea

One statement below expresses the main idea of the article. One statement is too general, or too broad. The other statement explains only part of the article; it is too narrow. Label the statements using the following key:

M—Main Idea   **B—Too Broad**   **N—Too Narrow**

_____ 1. Amanda Feilding believes that drilling a hole in her head has expanded her consciousness.

_____ 2. Trepanation has been performed for centuries.

_____ 3. Amanda Feilding made a video of herself undergoing trepanation.

_____ Score 15 points for a correct M answer.

_____ Score 5 points for each correct B or N answer.

_____ **Total Score:** Finding the Main Idea

B | Recalling Facts

How well do you remember the facts in the article? Put an X in the box next to the answer that correctly completes each statement about the article.

1. The earliest known instance of trepanation dates back
   - ☐ a. about 7,000 years.
   - ☐ b. to ancient Rome.
   - ☐ c. to the ancient people of Latin America.

2. Amanda Feilding first learned about trepanation from
   - ☐ a. Dr. Bart Huges.
   - ☐ b. Joey Mellen.
   - ☐ c. the Kissii tribe of western Kenya.

3. Dr. Huges believes that babies have a higher level of awareness because they have
   - ☐ a. undergone trepanation.
   - ☐ b. no worries or fears.
   - ☐ c. a soft spot on the top of their head.

4. The first time Mellen attempted trepanation, he
   - ☐ a. wrote a book about his experiences.
   - ☐ b. tried the procedure all by himself.
   - ☐ c. fainted and was taken to the hospital.

5. After Feilding drilled a hole through her head, she
   - ☐ a. passed out.
   - ☐ b. listened to music.
   - ☐ c. smiled.

Score 5 points for each correct answer.

_____ **Total Score:** Recalling Facts

C Making Inferences

When you combine your own experience and information from a text to draw a conclusion that is not directly stated in that text, you are making an inference. Below are five statements that may or may not be inferences based on information in the article. Label the statements using the following key:

C—Correct Inference   **F—Faulty Inference**

_____ 1. People who undergo trepanation risk grave damage and even death.

_____ 2. Everyone should undergo trepanation in order to reach a higher level of consciousness.

_____ 3. Dr. Huges was afraid to undergo trepanation.

_____ 4. Amanda Feilding has inspired many people to drill a hole in their head.

_____ 5. Feilding has a high tolerance for pain.

Score 5 points for each correct answer.

_____ **Total Score:** Making Inferences

D Using Words Precisely

Each numbered sentence below contains an underlined word or phrase from the article. Following the sentence are three definitions. One definition is closest to the meaning of the underlined word. One definition is opposite or nearly opposite. Label those two definitions using the following key. Do not label the remaining definition.

C—Closest   **O—Opposite or Nearly Opposite**

1. Feilding is not the first person to <u>subscribe to</u> this belief.

_____ a. discredit

_____ b. support

_____ c. publish

2. A second hole, this one more than three inches wide, had <u>partially</u> healed.

_____ a. completely

_____ b. beautifully

_____ c. in part

3. They have more <u>vivid</u> imaginations and a keener ability to perceive things.

_____ a. similar

_____ b. powerful

_____ c. ineffective

4. Although Huges <u>professed</u> confidence in his ideas, he didn't actually try trepanation himself.

_____ a. denied

_____ b. taught

_____ c. claimed

5. To ease their <u>anxieties</u>, she arranged to have Mellen film her as she trepanned herself.

_____ a. pain

_____ b. fearlessness

_____ c. worries

_____ Score 3 points for each correct C answer.

_____ Score 2 points for each correct O answer.

_____ **Total Score:** Using Words Precisely

Enter the four total scores in the spaces below, and add them together to find your Reading Comprehension Score. Then record your score on the graph on page 197.

Score	Question Type	Lesson 18
_____	Finding the Main Idea	
_____	Recalling Facts	
_____	Making Inferences	
_____	Using Words Precisely	
_____	**Reading Comprehension Score**	

Author's Approach

Put an X in the box next to the correct answer.

1. The main purpose of the first paragraph is to

☐ a. describe trepanation.

☐ b. introduce Amanda Feilding and her strange beliefs.

☐ c. convince the reader to undergo trepanation.

2. From the statement from the article "She thinks the world would be a happier place if more people drilled holes through their skulls," you can conclude that the author wants the reader to think that

☐ a. Amanda Feilding thinks differently from most people.

☐ b. Amanda Feilding is concerned about other people.

☐ c. Amanda Feilding is happier than most people.

3. Choose the statement below that best describes the author's position in paragraph 17.

☐ a. The author believes that Feilding should seek a Parliament seat again.

☐ b. The author believes that Feilding is needed in Parliament.

☐ c. The author believes that Feilding is too unconventional to serve effectively in public office.

_____ Number of correct answers

Record your personal assessment of your work on the Critical Thinking Chart on page 198.

Summarizing and Paraphrasing

Follow the directions provided for questions 1 and 2. Put an X in the box next to the correct answer for question 3.

1. Look for the important ideas and events in paragraphs 11 and 12. Summarize those paragraphs in one or two sentences.

_____

_____

_____

2. Complete the following one-sentence summary of the article using the lettered phrases from the phrase bank below. Write the letters on the lines.

Phrase Bank:
a. the history of trepanation
b. Feilding's efforts to convince others to undergo trepanation
c. Feilding's own experience with trepanation

After a short introduction, the article about Amanda Feilding begins with _____, goes on to explain _____, and ends with _____.

3. Read the statement about the article below. Then read the paraphrase of that statement. Choose the reason that best tells why the paraphrase does not say the same thing as the statement.

Statement: Feilding added a soundtrack of soothing music to the video she made of her trepanation procedure.

Paraphrase: Feilding played music to calm her nerves while she drilled a hole in her head.

☐ a. Paraphrase says too much.

☐ b. Paraphrase doesn't say enough.

☐ c. Paraphrase doesn't agree with the statement about the article.

_____ Number of correct answers

Record your personal assessment of your work on the Critical Thinking Chart on page 198.

Critical Thinking

Follow the directions provided for questions 1, 3, and 4. Put an X in the box next to the correct answer for the other questions.

1. For each statement below, write O if it expresses an opinion and write F if it expresses a fact.

_____ a. Some cultures have used trepanation for medical reasons or for spiritual purposes.

_____ b. Increasing the flow of blood to the brain makes a person more alert and insightful.

_____ c. Babies have more vivid imaginations than adults.

CRITICAL THINKING

2. Judging by events in the article, you can predict that the following will happen next:

☐ a. Amanda Feilding will be elected to Parliament.

☐ b. Amanda Feilding will convince Dr. Huges to drill a hole in his head.

☐ c. Amanda Feilding will continue to promote trepanation.

3. Choose from the letters below to correctly complete the following statement. Write the letters on the lines.

In the article, _____ and _____ are alike because they have both tried trepanation.

a. Amanda Feilding

b. Joey Mellon

c. Aulus Celsus

4. Think about cause-effect relationships in the article. Fill in the blanks in the cause-effect chart, drawing from the letters below.

Cause	Effect
Babies have soft spots in their skulls.	_____
_____	People who watch it faint.
Huges was frustrated that only a limited amount of blood can reach the brain.	_____

a. He searched for a way around this limitation.

b. The video of Feilding's trepanation procedure is very bloody.

c. They may have a higher level of consciousness than adults.

5. What did you have to do to answer question 3?

☐ a. find an opinion (what someone thinks about something)

☐ b. find a comparison (how things are the same)

☐ c. find a cause (why something happened)

_____ Number of correct answers

Record your personal assessment of your work on the Critical Thinking Chart on page 198.

Personal Response

What new question do you have about this topic?

_____

_____

_____

_____

Self-Assessment

When reading the article, I was having trouble with

_____

_____

_____

_____

CRITICAL THINKING

FERDINAND DEMARA
The Great Impostor

Ferdinand Waldo Demara, Jr. (right) used the credentials of Canadian surgeon Dr. Joseph C. Cyr (left) to enlist in the Canadian navy and work as a surgeon in the Korean War.

Dr. Joseph Cyr took a deep breath, then reached down into his patient's open chest wound and pulled out a bullet. He worked slowly and carefully after that. When he finally finished sewing up the man's chest, the attendants in the room cheered. They all congratulated Dr. Cyr for having successfully completed open-heart surgery. They might not have been so happy, however, if they had known the truth. Joseph Cyr was no doctor. He was an impostor—a person pretending to be someone whom he was not. His real name was Ferdinand W. Demara, and not only was he not a doctor, but also he had not even finished high school.

2   Ferdinand Demara was born in Lawrence, Massachusetts, in 1921. He was an extraordinarily bright boy, and schoolwork proved easy for him. In fact, in some ways it was too easy. Demara was bored. He needed something challenging to do, something bold and exciting and important. He believed that he was destined to lead a life of greatness. But there was little opportunity for greatness in the life of a Lawrence schoolboy. By the time Demara was fifteen, he felt he couldn't wait any longer. He had to get out and make his mark in the world. So one morning, instead of going to school,

Demara went to the railroad station and hopped a train out of town.

3   He spent the next several years trying to find the perfect outlet for his talents. He tried doing charity work and teaching at a Catholic boys' school. He even spent some time training to be a monk. But none of these endeavors worked out. Demara kept longing for something more glamorous. It occurred to him that soldiers had plenty of opportunities for glory and excitement. So in 1941, without a second thought, he joined the United States Army. It turned out, though, that a soldier's life was less dramatic than it appeared. Mostly it involved a lot of marching and taking orders and crawling through mud. After just a few weeks, Demara knew that the army would soon be missing one soldier.

4   To escape, he stole all the identification of a fellow soldier named Anthony Ignolia. He then simply walked off the army base and began life as Anthony Ignolia. Demara used the name for several months. By early 1942, though, he was feeling restless again. He still had visions of having a distinguished military career. Since World War II had broken out, he decided to try once again to serve his country. Under the name Fred W. Demara, he joined the U.S. Navy.

5   Within several weeks, Demara could see that the navy was just as dull as the army. After considering his options, he decided he might like to be a doctor. The navy's hospital school wouldn't take him, though, since he didn't even have a high school diploma. Demara fumed at the rejection. He knew how smart he was. In his heart, he knew he would make a brilliant doctor. For that matter, he knew he would make a brilliant military leader or professor or bishop. He simply didn't have the patience to go through the training. He couldn't stand the thought of spending years working his way up a career ladder. What he really wanted was just to wake up one day and *be* somebody important.

6   When Demara thought of it that way, suddenly it all seemed clear. He would steal the credentials of someone important, and pretend to be that person. That way he could reap the rewards of an exciting profession without going through years of tedious training. Demara searched a college catalog for the name of a faculty member who sounded interesting. He picked a man named Dr. Robert Linton French. French was a professor of psychology who had left teaching to fight in the war. Using personalized stationery with French's name on it, and a post office box address, Demara wrote for copies of French's credentials. Once he had them, he deserted the navy and assumed the identity of Dr. Robert Linton French.

7   Pretending to be a psychology professor required more effort than pretending to be Anthony Ignolia. Demara had to display poise, knowledge,

Ferdinand Waldo Demara, Jr., in 1952

and confidence. He succeeded beautifully. For two years he moved from town to town posing as Dr. French. Then, in the fall of 1945, he won a job as a dean at Gannon University in Pennsylvania. That appointment lasted over a year. Demara proved to be a popular teacher. He stayed one step ahead of his students by using every spare minute to read psychology books. Often he became so absorbed in studying that he would be late to class. He would burst into the classroom, look round in bewilderment, and ask, "What am I teaching?" The students thought it was a great joke. They didn't realize their professor was serious.

8   After a while, though, people began to get suspicious. So Demara sneaked out of town and moved on to new roles. He used stolen credentials to pose as a law student, a cancer researcher, and a zoologist.

9   Then in 1951 he finally got to be a doctor. He got his hands on the credentials of a surgeon named Joseph Cyr. Pretending to be Cyr, he joined the Royal Canadian Navy. He began performing operations, including the open-heart surgery that brought him such admiration. He completed that surgery on board a navy destroyer in the middle of the Korean combat zone. A storm had blown up, and the ship tossed and pitched furiously. Crew members strung up emergency lights in the commander's cabin. They then watched in awe as Dr. Cyr saved the life of a wounded Korean soldier.

10   It was one of Demara's finest moments. The Canadian press even ran a story about the doctor's heroic work. Unfortunately for Demara, the article ran in the hometown paper of the real Joseph Cyr. The doctor spoke up, and Demara suddenly found himself in police custody. Canadian officials were terribly embarrassed by the incident. They quickly sent Demara back to the United States.

11   For several years after that, Demara wandered around the United States under a variety of names. In the mid-1950s he obtained the credentials of a man named B. W. Jones. He went to Texas and used Jones's papers to land a job as a guard in the Huntsville maximum-security prison. He made a great impression and was soon promoted to assistant warden. Later he went to the small Maine village of North Haven, pretending to be a teacher named Martin Godgart. There he taught elementary school, became a Sea Scout leader, and played the local Santa Claus at Christmastime.

12   Eventually the law caught up with Demara. He was arrested in Maine for using a false identity. As usual, though, no one wanted to press charges. Even after learning about all his lies and all his tricks, people still liked Demara. One woman even wanted to marry him. While posing as Dr. Joseph Cyr, Demara had become engaged to a Canadian nurse. Even after learning that he was a fraud, she wrote him a letter declaring that she still loved him and would happily marry

him. She was not the only one who remained loyal to the "Great Impostor." Demara's crewmates from the Royal Canadian Navy still sent him an occasional Christmas card. The prison warden in Texas always spoke fondly of him. And the people of North Haven formed a committee for his defense.

13   Demara had several more adventures in his wild career as an impostor. He showed up in Mexico as an architect on a bridge construction project. He spent time in Alaska as a teacher at an Eskimo school. He even went to Cuba in hopes of running a prison there. In the end, though, Demara grew tired of his false, unsettled life. He gave up all his disguises and settled down in California under his real name. He spent his last years there, working as a counselor at a local hospital.

If you have been timed while reading this article, enter your reading time below. Then turn to the Words-per-Minute Table on page 195 and look up your reading speed (words per minute). Enter your reading speed on the graph on page 196.

Reading Time: Lesson 19

_____ : _____
Minutes   Seconds

A **Finding the Main Idea**

One statement below expresses the main idea of the article. One statement is too general, or too broad. The other statement explains only part of the article; it is too narrow. Label the statements using the following key:

M—Main Idea   **B—Too Broad**   **N—Too Narrow**

_____ 1. Ferdinand Demara was a brilliant impostor who successfully posed as a variety of professional people in highly responsible positions.

_____ 2. Ferdinand Demara was a very bright man whose desire for instant prestige led him to do all sorts of outrageous things.

_____ 3. Ferdinand Demara posed as a surgeon and successfully performed open-heart surgery.

_____ Score 15 points for a correct M answer.

_____ Score 5 points for each correct B or N answer.

_____ **Total Score:** Finding the Main Idea

B **Recalling Facts**

How well do you remember the facts in the article? Put an X in the box next to the answer that correctly completes each statement about the article.

1. Demara joined the United States Army because he
   ☐ a. was looking for glory and excitement.
   ☐ b. wanted to fight in Korea.
   ☐ c. enjoyed marching and drilling.

2. The navy's hospital school would not admit Demara because he
   ☐ a. had deserted the army.
   ☐ b. wasn't qualified.
   ☐ c. didn't have enough money to pay the tuition.

3. Demara saved the life of a wounded Korean soldier by
   ☐ a. bringing him to the home of Dr. Joseph Cyr.
   ☐ b. carrying him off the battlefield.
   ☐ c. performing open-heart surgery on him.

4. While posing as B. W. Jones in Texas, Demara
   ☐ a. fell in love with a nurse.
   ☐ b. became assistant warden of a prison.
   ☐ c. became an elementary school teacher.

5. When Demara was arrested in North Haven, Maine, the local citizens
   ☐ a. threatened to kill him.
   ☐ b. filed a suit against him.
   ☐ c. formed a committee for his defense.

_____ Score 5 points for each correct answer.

_____ **Total Score:** Recalling Facts

C Making Inferences

When you combine your own experience and information from a text to draw a conclusion that is not directly stated in that text, you are making an inference. Below are five statements that may or may not be inferences based on information in the article. Label the statements using the following key:

C—Correct Inference   F—Faulty Inference

_____ 1. Demara's hometown of Lawrence, Massachusetts, was not a very exciting place in the 1920s and 1930s.

_____ 2. Ferdinand Demara was an unfriendly person.

_____ 3. Ferdinand Demara enjoyed taking on new jobs.

_____ 4. Demara enjoyed physical work best.

_____ 5. Demara's fiancée did not care what Demara's true identity was.

Score 5 points for each correct answer.

_____ **Total Score:** Making Inferences

D Using Words Precisely

Each numbered sentence below contains an underlined word or phrase from the article. Following the sentence are three definitions. One definition is closest to the meaning of the underlined word. One definition is opposite or nearly opposite. Label those two definitions using the following key. Do not label the remaining definition.

C—Closest   O—Opposite or Nearly Opposite

1. He believed that he was <u>destined to</u> lead a life of greatness.

    _____ a. bound by fate to

    _____ b. never meant to

    _____ c. too smart to

2. He spent the next several years trying to find the perfect <u>outlet</u> for his talents.

    _____ a. identity

    _____ b. channel of expression

    _____ c. trap

3. He still had visions of having a <u>distinguished</u> military career.

    _____ a. inferior

    _____ b. retired

    _____ c. outstanding

4. That way he could reap the rewards of an exciting profession without going through the years of <u>tedious</u> training.

    _____ a. physically demanding

    _____ b. boring

    _____ c. interesting

5. They then watched in <u>awe</u> as Dr. Cyr saved the life of a wounded Korean soldier.

_____ a. curiosity

_____ b. calm acceptance

_____ c. amazement

_____ Score 3 points for each correct C answer.

_____ Score 2 points for each correct O answer.

_____ **Total Score:** Using Words Precisely

Enter the four total scores in the spaces below, and add them together to find your Reading Comprehension Score. Then record your score on the graph on page 197.

Score	Question Type	Lesson 19
_____	Finding the Main Idea	
_____	Recalling Facts	
_____	Making Inferences	
_____	Using Words Precisely	
_____	**Reading Comprehension Score**	

Author's Approach

Put an X in the box next to the correct answer.

1. The main purpose of the first paragraph is to
 ☐ a. introduce Ferdinand Demara as a surgeon.
 ☐ b. introduce Ferdinand Demara as an impostor.
 ☐ c. introduce Joseph Cyr as a surgeon.

2. What does the author imply by saying "After just a few weeks, Demara knew that the army would soon be missing one soldier"?
 ☐ a. Demara intended to get out of the army as soon as possible.
 ☐ b. Demara was a coward, afraid to stay in the army.
 ☐ c. Demara knew that the army was about to discharge him.

3. The author tells this story mainly by
 ☐ a. describing Demara's different careers.
 ☐ b. comparing Demara to real doctors, teachers, and soldiers.
 ☐ c. describing other people's impressions of Demara.

_____ Number of correct answers

Record your personal assessment of your work on the Critical Thinking Chart on page 198.

CRITICAL THINKING

Summarizing and Paraphrasing

Put an X in the box next to the correct answer for questions 1 and 3. Follow the directions provided for the other question.

1. Below are summaries of the article. Choose the summary that says all the most important things about the article but in the fewest words.

☐ a. Ferdinand Demara assumed the identity of many people. Eventually, he grew tired of his disguises and settled down in California.

☐ b. Some of Ferdinand Demara's identities included that of a doctor, soldier, professor, and prison guard. When he was finally caught and arrested for using a false identity, the people he had worked with didn't want to press charges.

☐ c. Although he never finished high school, Ferdinand Demara successfully posed as an expert in many different careers. Even after he had been exposed as a fraud, most of the people he had fooled supported him.

2. Reread paragraph 9 in the article. Below, write a summary of the paragraph in no more than 25 words.

_____

_____

_____

Reread your summary and decide whether it covers the important ideas in the paragraph. Next, decide how to shorten the summary to 15 words or less without leaving out any essential information. Write this summary below.

_____

_____

_____

3. Choose the sentence that correctly restates the following sentence from the article:

"He stayed one step ahead of his students by using every spare minute to read psychology books."

☐ a. Demara always ran ahead of his students.

☐ b. Demara used all of his free time for running and reading psychology books.

☐ c. By constantly reading and studying psychology in his spare time, Demara managed to know just a little more than his students.

_____ Number of correct answers

Record your personal assessment of your work on the Critical Thinking Chart on page 198.

Critical Thinking

Put an X in the box next to the correct answer for questions 1 and 3. Follow the directions provided for the other questions.

1. From what the article told about Ferdinand Demara, you can predict that he

☐ a. would have finished school if he had grown up in a larger town because there he would have admired the teachers.

☐ b. would have made an excellent actor or spy because of his ability to convince people he was someone else.

☐ c. would have gone on being an impostor if he hadn't been caught.

2. Choose from the letters below to correctly complete the following statement. Write the letters on the lines.

According to the article, _____ caused Ferdinand Demara to _____, and the effect was _____.

a. he assumed another man's identity

b. long for something more exciting

c. the dull life of the army

3. Of the following theme categories, which would this story fit into?

☐ a. science fiction

☐ b. love stories

☐ c. true-life adventures

4. Which paragraphs from the article provide evidence that supports your answer to question 2?

_____ Number of correct answers

Record your personal assessment of your work on the Critical Thinking Chart on page 198.

Personal Response

I know the feeling

_____

_____

_____

_____

Self-Assessment

A word or phrase in the article that I do not understand is

_____

_____

_____

_____

CRITICAL THINKING

DENNIS RODMAN
Bad as He Wants to Be

When Dennis Rodman puts on his basketball uniform, his fans can expect one thing: he will rebound like a demon. He can't shoot from outside very well, and he doesn't dribble the ball much. But Rodman doesn't have to do either of those things. His job is to get the ball. He has helped his team by leading the National Basketball Association in rebounds year after year. Even though he is smaller than many of the players, some people say that Dennis Rodman is the best NBA rebounder ever.

2   Aside from his superb rebounding skills, however, Rodman is completely unpredictable. No one ever knows what he will do next. He changes the color of his hair for every game. Some nights it is neon green; other times it's snow white. Over the course of his long career, he has experimented with just about every color combination possible. On some occasions, he even shows up with his team's logo spray-painted on his hair.

3   If Rodman's hair color doesn't grab your attention, his wide range of body tattoos will. He completes his ensemble with an eclectic assortment of ear and nose rings. Simply put, Rodman is quite a

Chicago Bulls forward Dennis Rodman celebrates in the NBA finals in 1996.

sight. And that is just what he intends to be.

4   Off the court, Rodman can be just as bizarre. In 1996, he wrote his autobiography, *Bad As I Wanna Be*. Tens of thousands of new books are published every year. In such a competitive field, it's hard for most writers to get people's attention, but that has never been a problem for Rodman. He knew exactly how to grab the limelight. At a book signing in Chicago, he arrived on a motorcycle with his hair dyed silver. He was wearing makeup, leather pants, and a pink feather boa.

5   Later, in New York City, Rodman went even further, arriving at a Barnes & Noble bookstore in a horse-drawn carriage with a police escort. He was dressed in a white bridal gown, complete with veil and long white gloves. He had made up his face to look like a woman's. And, for the final touch, Rodman wore a blonde wig. When someone asked him if he was going to get married, he teasingly replied, "Oh, yes, I'm so thrilled." Rodman got what he wanted—publicity. *Bad As I Wanna Be* made it to the *New York Times* bestseller list and stayed there for many weeks.

6   Rodman's antics upset many people. They complain that he isn't exactly the role model they expect a professional athlete to be. But Rodman refuses to alter his behavior to please the public. "I paint my fingernails. I color my hair. I sometimes wear women's clothes," he announced in his autobiography. "I want to challenge people's image of what an athlete is supposed to be." As defiant as ever, he went on to declare, "I'm always looking

Dressed as a bride, Rodman poses with "bridesmaids" at a book signing.

for new ways to test myself. There are no rules, no boundaries."

7   This aspect of Rodman's character might be dismissed as all show, but there is a darker, more desperate side to him as well. In his own peculiar way, Rodman was driven to succeed. His father abandoned the family when Rodman was just a boy, and his mother favored his two sisters over him. Rodman was a shy, skinny kid who was cut from his high school football team and quit the basketball team because he didn't get much playing time. Later, he was jailed for stealing watches. "In that cell, I swore I was going to make something of myself," he later recalled.

8   By age 20, Rodman's body had matured; he measured 6' 8" tall and weighed 210 pounds. More importantly, he had learned to love the game of basketball. Earlier he had been a mediocre player, but now he blossomed into greatness. Allen Steinberg described the transformation in his book *Rebound: The Dennis Rodman Story:* "He picked [basketball] up like that, as though a spell had been cast with a wand. Where he used to blunder, he now glided and soared. Moves came as natural to him now as they'd felt clumsy before."

9   Rodman showed enough talent to win a college scholarship at Cooke County Junior College. But he was no scholar, and he soon flunked out. Luckily, he got a second chance, and this time he didn't waste it. He got into Southeastern

Oklahoma State University, where he won All-American honors three times. In 1986, he was drafted by the NBA's Detroit Pistons. Still, Rodman wondered whether he would succeed in the pros. He later said that he was "nobody from nowhere with nothing."

10   Rodman did make it. He doesn't score much, but he can play tough defense, often shutting down the other team's best players. And he can grab rebounds by the bushel. His play has helped both the Detroit Pistons and the Chicago Bulls win several NBA titles.

11   As Rodman became a star, he also started getting under people's skin. Fans in other towns hate him. Rodman dismisses their complaints with a shrug. "People love to hate Dennis Rodman," he said about himself, "but once he's on their team, they love Dennis Rodman."

12   In fact, it isn't just the opposing teams fans that grumble about Rodman; his bizarre actions on and off the basketball court upset his own fans and sometimes even his own teammates. People condemn him for playing dirty, committing flagrant fouls, and starting fights. As a result of his outrageous behavior, Rodman has been ejected from many games. As he walks off the court, he rips off his shirt and flings it into the crowd. His frequent ejections have done nothing to help his team's chances of winning.

13   Of course, other players occasionally get ejected, too, but Rodman always goes further than anyone else. He is like a

ticking time bomb on the court. During one game in 1996, he used his head to butt a referee. As a result, he was suspended by the league for six games and fined $20,000. Another time he kicked a photographer during a game. Again, NBA officials suspended him.

16   People have begun to wonder just how crazy Rodman really is. He has been ejected, suspended, and fined over and over again. At one point league officials even told him he had to get counseling.

17   Is it all just an act? It's hard to know for sure. But Rodman clearly loves playing the role of the "bad guy." And he plays it very well. Once, in the middle of his career, he said, "I'm not an athlete anymore, I'm an entertainer."

If you have been timed while reading this article, enter your reading time below. Then turn to the Words-per-Minute Table on page 195 and look up your reading speed (words per minute). Enter your reading speed on the graph on page 196.

Reading Time: Lesson 20

_____ : _____
Minutes   Seconds

A Finding the Main Idea

One statement below expresses the main idea of the article. One statement is too general, or too broad. The other statement explains only part of the article; it is too narrow. Label the statements using the following key:

M—Main Idea   **B—Too Broad**   **N—Too Narrow**

_____ 1. Dennis Rodman's flamboyant behavior on and off the basketball court entertains and angers fans and players.

_____ 2. Many people are upset by Dennis Rodman's antics.

_____ 3. Dennis Rodman arrived at a book signing in New York City dressed in a bridal gown and wig.

_____ Score 15 points for a correct M answer.

_____ Score 5 points for each correct B or N answer.

_____ **Total Score:** Finding the Main Idea

B Recalling Facts

How well do you remember the facts in the article? Put an X in the box next to the answer that correctly completes each statement about the article.

1. Year after year, Dennis Rodman has led the National Basketball Association in
   ☐ a. rebounding.
   ☐ b. dribbling.
   ☐ c. shooting.

2. Rodman helped promote his autobiography *Bad as I Wanna Be* by
   ☐ a. getting married during a book signing.
   ☐ b. getting arrested.
   ☐ c. arriving at book signings dressed in outrageous outfits.

3. In high school, Rodman
   ☐ a. was a star basketball player.
   ☐ b. was a talented football player.
   ☐ c. did not distinguish himself as an athlete.

4. Rodman was drafted by the Detroit Pistons
   ☐ a. in 1996.
   ☐ b. in 1986.
   ☐ c. after he had played for the Chicago Bulls.

5. The NBA suspended Rodman and fined him $20,000 for
   ☐ a. committing a flagrant foul.
   ☐ b. ripping off his shirt and flinging it to the crowd.
   ☐ c. head-butting a referee.

Score 5 points for each correct answer.

_____ **Total Score:** Recalling Facts

C | Making Inferences

When you combine your own experience and information from a text to draw a conclusion that is not directly stated in that text, you are making an inference. Below are five statements that may or may not be inferences based on information in the article. Label the statements using the following key:

C—Correct Inference   **F—Faulty Inference**

_____ 1. Dennis Rodman has always been outstanding at any sport he tried.

_____ 2. Rodman's bizarre behavior is meant to compensate for his lack of talent on the basketball court.

_____ 3. The best NBA rebounders are usually the tallest members of the team.

_____ 4. Rodman had a difficult childhood.

_____ 5. Some people probably buy tickets to NBA games just to see Rodman's antics on the court.

Score 5 points for each correct answer.

_____ **Total Score:** Making Inferences

D | Using Words Precisely

Each numbered sentence below contains an underlined word or phrase from the article. Following the sentence are three definitions. One definition is closest to the meaning of the underlined word. One definition is opposite or nearly opposite. Label those two definitions using the following key. Do not label the remaining definition.

C—Closest   **O—Opposite or Nearly Opposite**

1. Aside from his superb rebounding skills, however, Rodman is completely <u>unpredictable</u>.

_____ a. without talent

_____ b. surprising

_____ c. expected

2. But Rodman refuses to <u>alter</u> his behavior to please the public.

_____ a. change

_____ b. discuss

_____ c. preserve

3. Earlier he had been a <u>mediocre</u> player, but now he blossomed into greatness.

_____ a. average

_____ b. exceptional

_____ c. professional

4. People condemn him for playing dirty, committing <u>flagrant</u> fouls, and starting fights.

_____ a. restrained

_____ b. memorable

_____ c. glaringly bad

5. As a result of his outrageous behavior, Rodman has been <u>ejected</u> from many games.

_____ a. applauded

_____ b. thrown out

_____ c. retained

_____ Score 3 points for each correct C answer.

_____ Score 2 points for each correct O answer.

_____ **Total Score:** Using Words Precisely

Enter the four total scores in the spaces below, and add them together to find your Reading Comprehension Score. Then record your score on the graph on page 197.

Score	Question Type	Lesson 20
_____	Finding the Main Idea	
_____	Recalling Facts	
_____	Making Inferences	
_____	Using Words Precisely	
_____	**Reading Comprehension Score**	

Author's Approach

Put an X in the box next to the correct answer.

1. The author uses the first sentence of the article to

☐ a. inform the reader about Rodman's antics on the basketball court.

☐ b. describe Rodman's skill as a basketball player.

☐ c. compare Dennis Rodman to a demon.

2. Which of the following statements from the article best describes Dennis Rodman's early years?

☐ a. "Rodman was a shy, skinny kid who was cut from his high school football team and quit the basketball team because he didn't get much playing time."

☐ b. "Aside from his superb rebounding skills, however, Rodman is completely unpredictable."

☐ c. "He was wearing makeup, leather pants, and a pink feather boa."

3. Choose the statement below that is the weakest argument for claiming that Dennis Rodman is a good role model for young fans.

☐ a. He is one of the best rebounders ever to play in the NBA.

☐ b. He doesn't shoot very well or dribble the ball much.

☐ c. He has trouble controlling his behavior on the basketball court.

4. The author probably wrote this article in order to

☐ a. describe Dennis Rodman's outstanding athletic ability.

☐ b. express a negative opinion about men who dress like women.

☐ c. provide insight into Dennis Rodman's character.

_____ Number of correct answers

Record your personal assessment of your work on the Critical Thinking Chart on page 198.

CRITICAL THINKING

Summarizing and Paraphrasing

Follow the directions provided for question 1. Put an X in the box next to the correct answer for question 2.

1. Reread paragraph 7 in the article. Below, write a summary of the paragraph in no more than 25 words.

_____

_____

_____

_____

Reread your summary and decide whether it covers the important ideas in the paragraph. Next, decide how to shorten the summary to 15 words or less without leaving out any essential information. Write this summary below.

_____

_____

2. Choose the best one-sentence paraphrase for the following sentence from the article:

    "In fact, it isn't just the opposing team's fans that grumble about Rodman; his bizarre actions on and off the basketball court upset his own fans and sometimes even his own teammates."

    ☐ a.   The opposing team's fans complain about Rodman's behavior.

    ☐ b.   Rodman's teammates become upset when the fans complain about his behavior.

    ☐ c.   Fans and players of his own team have joined others in complaining about Rodman's behavior.

_____ Number of correct answers

Record your personal assessment of your work on the Critical Thinking Chart on page 198.

Critical Thinking

Put an X in the box next to the correct answer for questions 1, 2, and 5. Follow the directions provided for the other questions.

1. Which of the following statements from the article is an opinion rather than a fact?

    ☐ a.   "He changes the color of his hair for every game."

    ☐ b.   "Dennis Rodman is the best NBA rebounder ever."

    ☐ c.   "*Bad As I Wanna Be* made it to the *New York Times* bestseller list and stayed there for many weeks."

2. Judging by what Dennis Rodman said, you can predict that he will

    ☐ a.   continue to try to entertain people.

    ☐ b.   concentrate on improving his athletic skills.

    ☐ c.   get married soon.

CRITICAL THINKING

3. Choose from the letters below to correctly complete the following statement. Write the letters on the lines.

In the article, _____ and _____ are different.

a. Rodman's basketball skills in high school

b. Rodman's basketball skills as a Detroit Piston

c. Rodman's basketball skills as a Chicago Bull

4. Read paragraph 9. Then choose from the letters below to correctly complete the following statement. Write the letters on the lines.

According to paragraph 9, _____ because _____.

a. Rodman flunked out of Cooke County Junior College

b. he was drafted by the Detroit Pistons

c. his grades weren't good enough

5. If you were an athlete who hoped to play in the NBA someday, how could you use the information in the article to improve your game?

☐ a. Like Dennis Rodman, develop and perfect a particular skill.

☐ b. Like Dennis Rodman, behave outrageously on and off the court.

☐ c. Like Dennis Rodman, write your autobiography.

_____ Number of correct answers

Record your personal assessment of your work on the Critical Thinking Chart on page 198.

Personal Response

If I were the author, I would add

_____

_____

_____

_____

because

_____

_____

_____

_____

Self-Assessment

Before reading this article, I already knew

_____

_____

_____

_____

IMELDA MARCOS
World's Greatest Shopper

A small part of the famous shoe collection of Imelda Marcos

The lady loves to shop. The old saying "shop 'til you drop" fits her like one of her Gucci gloves. One afternoon she flew off to Switzerland and spent $12 million on jewelry without batting an eye. At luxury hotels, she tossed around $100 tips like confetti. She gave one doorman a Cartier watch worth thousands of dollars. But she could afford it. At one time she was thought to be the richest woman in the world.

2   Her name is Imelda Marcos. Her husband was Ferdinand Marcos, president of the Philippines. Imelda wasn't always rich. In fact, she was born into poverty. Imelda's mother raised her five children in a broken-down garage. One cousin remembers that the family "slept together on long boards propped up by milk boxes."

3   But as a young woman, Imelda had two things going for her: a sharp mind and good looks. She entered beauty contests and attracted the attention of many young men. In 1954, she met Ferdinand Marcos, a wealthy politician. Ferdinand took Imelda to his bank and showed her his private vault. Imelda's eyes popped wide open at the piles of U.S. dollar bills he had stashed there. She was

suddenly convinced that she had met the man of her dreams. After a whirlwind romance that lasted just 11 days, Imelda and Ferdinand were married.

4   Nine years later, Ferdinand Marcos was elected president of the Philippines. For the next 20 years, he and Imelda steadily plundered their nation's riches. They denied doing any such thing, of course. Yet experts point out that their net worth reached about $10 billion. So how did they rack up such massive wealth? After all, Imelda did not work, and Ferdinand made only $5,700 a year as head of the country.

5   The high times came to an end in 1986. The Filipinos wanted a new leader and elected Corazon Aquino president. But Ferdinand did not go quietly. In an effort to stay in power, he declared a state of emergency. By that time, though, he had lost all political support. On February 26, 1986, he and Imelda were forced to flee the country.

6   Only then did the Philippine citizens see the real Imelda. She and her husband took as much as they could with them. Still, they left behind evidence of Imelda's mindless greed. In one room of their palace, investigators found three thousand pairs of shoes. All were size 8½, and all belonged to Imelda. Investigators also found 500 bras (mostly black), 1,500 handbags, and rack after rack of fur coats and evening gowns.

7   People around the world were shocked at the depth of Imelda's avarice. She became a laughingstock. One joke went like this. Question: What was Imelda's favorite industry? Answer: Mining. ("That's mine, that's mine, that's mine.")

8   Old friends told unbelievable stories about Imelda's spending habits. Each one seemed more incredible than the last. In 1979, for example, Imelda opened up a new beach resort and invited her rich friends to attend. But at the last minute, she decided that the sand wasn't white enough. So she sent a plane to Australia to pick up a load of white sand.

9   Another time she had just taken off from Rome in her jet. To her horror, she discovered that there was no cheese on the plane. Did she do without? Of course not—she was Imelda Marcos. She ordered the plane back to Rome to pick up some cheese.

10   For her daughter's wedding, Imelda went even further overboard. The wedding took place in the small Philippine town of Sarrat. The town wasn't quite up to Imelda's standards so she had a new luxury hotel built, as well as a new airport. Then she had the homes in the town remodeled to resemble 17th-century Spanish villas. She also reserved 500 first-class cabins on an ocean liner for the wedding guests. The price for all this was $10.3 million.

Former beauty queen and first lady of the Philippines Imelda Marcos in 1985

11   Imelda's wild shopping sprees were the stuff of legend. She hopped from Rome to Tokyo to New York in her private jet with its built-in shower and gold bathroom fixtures. When she walked through the front door of a boutique, the owner must have smiled knowing that sales receipts were about to take a massive leap.

12   Imelda didn't just buy a nice dress; she bought a rack or two. If she liked a particular blouse, she would buy ten dozen. If she didn't like a blouse all that much, she might buy only five dozen. In bookstores, she would purchase every third book on the shelves. Sometimes it was every other book. High-quality leather-bound books stood absolutely no chance: Imelda would buy them all. And, naturally, she loaded up on pricey jewelry, expensive watches, and fine paintings. Most of the time, she paid in crisp American dollars. Imelda had a maid whose sole job was to iron dollar bills.

13   Imelda lived in a dream world, with a fantasy view of her country and of herself. The Philippines was and is one of the poorest nations in the world. Many Filipinos live in abject poverty, yet Imelda was blind to that fact. "In the Philippines we live in a paradise," she once boasted.

"There are no poor [people] like there are in other countries."

14   Imelda, the former beauty queen, felt that she always had to look perfect. After all, she reasoned, she had an image to maintain. The hairstyle, the clothing, the jewelry, the makeup all had to be flawlessly coordinated. "I am my little people's star and slave," she once declared. "When I go out into the barrios [poor areas], I get dressed up because I know the little people want to see a star."

15   Imelda couldn't grasp why some people believed she was dishonest. "They call me corrupt," she complained. "I would not look like this if I am corrupt," she continued, while admiring herself. "Some ugliness would settle down on my system." Apparently, in Imelda's mixed-up mind, all crooks had to be ugly.

16   Imelda's fall from power didn't put her in the poorhouse. She and Ferdinand, who died in 1989, stashed millions in banks around the world. Since 1986, the Filipinos have been trying to retrieve the loot. They have recovered some, but vast sums are still unaccounted for.

17   Meanwhile, Imelda's grip on reality hasn't improved. In 1991, she returned to her home country to face charges of

corruption. "I come home penniless," she pleaded. She was, of course, far from destitute. When the police took her fingerprints, one finger sported an 11-carat diamond. Also, Imelda had chartered a 747 jet plane for her flight back to the Philippines. The cost of the plane was $600,000. Imelda Marcos is no longer the First Lady of the Philippines. But she remains one of the world's all-time great spenders. ✖

If you have been timed while reading this article, enter your reading time below. Then turn to the Words-per-Minute Table on page 195 and look up your reading speed (words per minute). Enter your reading speed on the graph on page 196.

Reading Time: Lesson 21

_____ : _____
Minutes   Seconds

A │ Finding the Main Idea

One statement below expresses the main idea of the article. One statement is too general, or too broad. The other statement explains only part of the article; it is too narrow. Label the statements using the following key:

M—Main Idea   **B—Too Broad**   **N—Too Narrow**

_____ 1. While many Filipinos lived in poverty, Imelda Marcos enjoyed great luxury.

_____ 2. When Ferdinand and Imelda Marcos fled the Philippines, Imelda left behind three thousand pairs of shoes.

_____ 3. While her husband was president of the Philippines, Imelda Marcos helped him plunder their nation's riches and mindlessly spend millions of dollars.

_____ Score 15 points for a correct M answer.

_____ Score 5 points for each correct B or N answer.

_____ **Total Score:** Finding the Main Idea

B │ Recalling Facts

How well do you remember the facts in the article? Put an X in the box next to the answer that correctly completes each statement about the article.

1. During the 20-year presidency of Ferdinand Marcos, he and Imelda
   ☐ a. accumulated massive wealth.
   ☐ b. got married.
   ☐ c. met at a beauty contest.

2. Ferdinand Marcos declared a state of emergency after
   ☐ a. the Filipinos saw the real Imelda.
   ☐ b. investigators found evidence of Imelda's mindless greed.
   ☐ c. the Filipinos elected Corazon Aquino president.

3. In preparation for her daughter's wedding in the small town of Sarrat, Imelda
   ☐ a. flew to Rome to buy some cheese.
   ☐ b. sent a plane to Australia to pick up a load of white sand.
   ☐ c. had a new hotel and airport built.

4. Imelda had a maid whose sole job was to
   ☐ a. shop for books.
   ☐ b. iron dollar bills.
   ☐ c. always look perfect.

5. In 1991, Imelda returned to the Philippines and
   ☐ a. returned vast sums of her country's money.
   ☐ b. once again became First Lady of the Philippines.
   ☐ c. claimed that she was penniless.

Score 5 points for each correct answer.

_____ **Total Score:** Recalling Facts

C | Making Inferences

When you combine your own experience and information from a text to draw a conclusion that is not directly stated in that text, you are making an inference. Below are five statements that may or may not be inferences based on information in the article. Label the statements using the following key:

C—Correct Inference   **F—Faulty Inference**

_____ 1. The only reason Imelda Marcos bought lots of leather-bound books was because she loved to read.

_____ 2. Imelda felt guilty about living a luxurious lifestyle while many Filipinos lived in poverty.

_____ 3. During all of Ferdinand's presidency, the Philippine people knew that he and Imelda were growing rich on their money.

_____ 4. Imelda spared no expense for herself or for her family and friends.

_____ 5. One of the reasons Imelda married Ferdinand was her desire to access his money.

Score 5 points for each correct answer.

_____ **Total Score:** Making Inferences

D | Using Words Precisely

Each numbered sentence below contains an underlined word or phrase from the article. Following the sentence are three definitions. One definition is closest to the meaning of the underlined word. One definition is opposite or nearly opposite. Label those two definitions using the following key. Do not label the remaining definition.

C—Closest   O—Opposite or Nearly Opposite

1. After a <u>whirlwind</u> romance that lasted just 11 days, Imelda and Ferdinand were married.

_____ a. very speedy

_____ b. confusing

_____ c. sluggish

2. For the next 20 years, he and Imelda steadily <u>plundered</u> their nations riches.

_____ a. added to

_____ b. counted

_____ c. ransacked

3. People around the world were shocked at the depth of Imelda's <u>avarice</u>.

_____ a. stupidity

_____ b. greed

_____ c. selflessness

4. Many Filipinos live in <u>abject</u> poverty, yet Imelda was blind to that fact.

_____ a. dignified

_____ b. relative

_____ c. degraded

5. She was, of course, far from <u>destitute</u>.

_____ a. wealthy

_____ b. penniless

_____ c. honest

_____ Score 3 points for each correct C answer.

_____ Score 2 points for each correct O answer.

_____ **Total Score:** Using Words Precisely

Enter the four total scores in the spaces below, and add them together to find your Reading Comprehension Score. Then record your score on the graph on page 197.

Score	Question Type	Lesson 21
_____	Finding the Main Idea	
_____	Recalling Facts	
_____	Making Inferences	
_____	Using Words Precisely	
_____	**Reading Comprehension Score**	

Author's Approach

Put an X in the box next to the correct answer.

1. What is the author's purpose in writing "Imelda Marcos: World's Greatest Shopper"?

☐ a. To express an opinion about Imelda's out-of-control greed

☐ b. To express admiration for Imelda's shopping abilities

☐ c. To emphasize the similarities between Ferdinand and Imelda Marcos

2. Which of the following statements from the article best describes Imelda Marcos during the years she was the First Lady of the Philippines?

☐ a. "In fact, she was born into poverty."

☐ b. "But as a young woman, Imelda had two things going for her: a sharp mind and good looks."

☐ c. "The lady loves to shop."

3. What does the author imply by saying in paragraph 3 that "She was suddenly convinced that she had met the man of her dreams"?

☐ a. Imelda decided to fall in love with Ferdinand Marcos because of his money.

☐ b. Imelda realized that she had dreamed about Ferdinand Marcos.

☐ c. Imelda realized that she truly loved Ferdinand Marcos because of his goodness and kindness.

4. Choose the statement below that best describes the author's position in paragraph 15.

☐ a. Imelda is beautiful but misunderstood.

☐ b. Imelda is a vain woman who is out of touch with reality.

☐ c. Imelda believes that all ugly people are crooks.

_____ Number of correct answers

Record your personal assessment of your work on the Critical Thinking Chart on page 198.

CRITICAL THINKING

Summarizing and Paraphrasing

Follow the directions provided for questions 1 and 2. Put an X in the box next to the correct answer for question 3.

1. Complete the following one-sentence summary of the article using the lettered phrases from the phrase bank below. Write the letters on the lines.

> **Phrase Bank:**
> a. Imelda's early years and her marriage to Ferdinand
> b. Imelda Marcos's spending habits during her husband's presidency
> c. her refusal to admit her corruption

After the introductory paragraph, the article about Imelda Marcos describes _____, goes on to explain _____, and ends with _____.

2. Reread paragraph 12 in the article. Below, write a summary of the paragraph in no more than 25 words.

_____

_____

_____

Reread your summary and decide whether it covers the important ideas in the paragraph. Next, try to shorten the summary to 15 words or less without leaving out any essential information. Write this summary below.

_____

_____

_____

3. Read the statement about the article below. Then read the paraphrase of that statement. Choose the reason that best tells why the paraphrase does not say the same thing as the statement.

Statement: Imelda Marcos not only loved to buy and wear expensive things, but she also loved the power she derived from spending lots of money.

Paraphrase: Imelda Marcos loved to wear expensive clothes and spend a great deal of money.

☐ a.   Paraphrase says too much.

☐ b.   Paraphrase doesn't say enough.

☐ c.   Paraphrase doesn't agree with the statement about the article.

> _____ Number of correct answers
>
> Record your personal assessment of your work on the Critical Thinking Chart on page 198.

Critical Thinking

Put an X in the box next to the correct answer for questions 1 and 4. Follow the directions provided for the other questions.

1. Judging by what Imelda Marcos said, you can predict that she will

☐ a.   never admit to any wrongdoing.

☐ b.   become the slave of the Philippine people.

☐ c.   return the money she took from the Philippines.

2. Choose from the letters below to correctly complete the following statement. Write the letters on the lines.

In the article, _____ and _____ are alike because they both were presidents of the Philippines.

a.   Imelda Marcos

b.   Corazon Aquino

c.   Ferdinand Marcos

3. Think about cause–effect relationships in the article. Fill in the blanks in the cause–effect chart, drawing from the letters below.

Cause	Effect
Sarrat wasn't up to Imelda's standards.	_____
Imelda had to uphold her image.	_____
_____	Imelda married Ferdinand Marcos.

a.   Imelda saw the contents of Marcos's private vault.

b.   Imelda had the homes in the town remodeled.

c.   Imelda's appearance always had to be perfect.

4. Of the following theme categories, which would this story fit into?

☐ a.   Leaders always have their people's best interests at heart.

☐ b.   Money and power corrupt.

☐ c.   Growing up poor gives you a kind and generous spirit.

_____ Number of correct answers

Record your personal assessment of your work on the Critical Thinking Chart on page 198.

Personal Response

I agree with the author because

_____

_____

_____

_____

Self-Assessment

While reading the article, I found it easiest to

_____

_____

_____

_____

Compare and Contrast

Think about the articles you read in Unit Three. Choose four articles that describe the eccentrics whom you would most like to meet. Write the titles of those articles in the first column of the chart below. Use information from the articles to fill in the empty boxes of the chart.

Title	Where and when did this person live?	How did this person feel about himself or herself?	What would be the first question you would ask this person if you met?

Think of someone on the current scene whom you consider to be an eccentric. Explain why you think that person is eccentric. _____

_____

_____

Words-per-Minute Table

Unit Three

Directions: If you were timed while reading an article, refer to the Reading Time you recorded in the box at the end of the article. Use this words-per-minute table to determine your reading speed for that article. Then plot your reading speed on the graph on page 196.

Lesson No. of Words	15 1460	16 1129	17 1240	18 1051	19 1336	20 1091	21 1131	
1:30	973	752	827	701	891	727	754	**90**
1:40	876	677	744	631	802	655	679	**100**
1:50	796	616	676	573	729	595	617	**110**
2:00	730	564	620	526	668	546	566	**120**
2:10	674	521	572	485	617	504	522	**130**
2:20	626	484	531	450	573	468	485	**140**
2:30	584	452	496	420	534	436	452	**150**
2:40	548	423	465	394	501	409	424	**160**
2:50	515	398	438	371	472	385	399	**170**
3:00	487	376	413	350	445	364	377	**180**
3:10	461	356	392	332	422	345	357	**190**
3:20	438	339	372	315	401	327	339	**200**
3:30	417	323	354	300	382	312	323	**210**
3:40	398	308	338	287	364	298	308	**220**
3:50	381	294	323	274	349	285	295	**230**
4:00	365	282	310	263	334	273	283	**240**
4:10	350	271	298	252	321	262	271	**250**
4:20	337	260	286	243	308	252	261	**260**
4:30	324	251	276	234	297	242	251	**270**
4:40	313	242	266	225	286	234	242	**280**
4:50	302	233	257	217	276	226	234	**290**
5:00	292	226	248	210	267	218	226	**300**
5:10	283	218	240	203	259	211	219	**310**
5:20	274	212	233	197	251	205	212	**320**
5:30	265	205	225	191	243	198	206	**330**
5:40	258	199	219	185	236	193	200	**340**
5:50	250	193	213	180	229	187	194	**350**
6:00	243	188	207	175	223	182	189	**360**
6:10	237	183	201	170	217	177	183	**370**
6:20	231	178	196	166	211	172	179	**380**
6:30	225	173	191	162	206	168	174	**390**
6:40	219	169	186	158	200	164	170	**400**
6:50	214	165	181	154	196	160	166	**410**
7:00	209	161	177	150	191	156	162	**420**
7:10	204	158	173	147	186	152	158	**430**
7:20	199	154	169	143	182	149	154	**440**
7:30	195	150	165	140	178	145	151	**450**
7:40	190	147	162	137	174	142	148	**460**
7:50	186	144	158	134	171	139	144	**470**
8:00	183	141	155	131	167	136	141	**480**

Minutes and Seconds

Seconds

Plotting Your Progress: Reading Speed

Unit Three

Directions: If you were timed while reading an article, write your words-per-minute rate for that in the box under the number of the lesson. Then plot your reading speed on the graph by putting a small X on the line directly above the number of the lesson, across from the number of words per minute you read. As you mark your speed for each lesson, graph your progress by drawing a line to connect the X's.

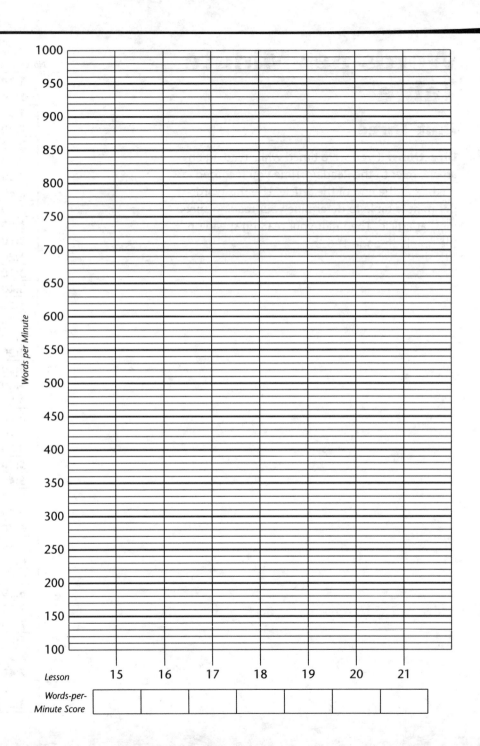

Plotting Your Progress: Reading Comprehension

Unit Three

Directions: Write your Reading Comprehension score for each lesson in the box under the number of the lesson. Then plot your score on the graph by putting a small X on the line directly above the number of the lesson and across from the score you earned. As you mark your score for each lesson, graph your progress by drawing a line to connect the X's.

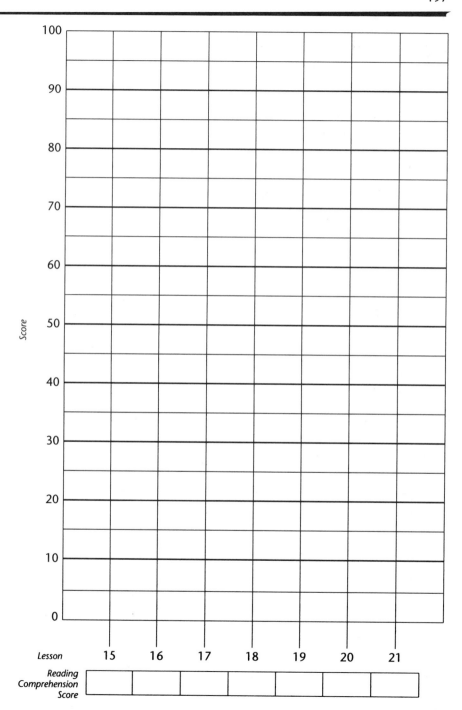

Score

Lesson	15	16	17	18	19	20	21
Reading Comprehension Score							

Plotting Your Progress: Critical Thinking

Unit Three

Directions: Work with your teacher to evaluate your responses to the Critical Thinking questions for each lesson. Then fill in the appropriate spaces in the chart below. For each lesson and each type of Critical Thinking question, do the following: Mark a minus sign (–) in the box to indicate areas in which you feel you could improve. Mark a plus sign (+) to indicate areas in which you feel you did well. Mark a minus-slash-plus sign (–/+) to indicate areas in which you had mixed success. Then write any comments you have about your performance, including ideas for improvement.

Lesson	Author's Approach	Summarizing and Paraphrasing	Critical Thinking
15			
16			
17			
18			
19			
20			
21			

Picture Credits

Cover: Photo montage by Karen Christoffersen

Sample Lesson: pp. 3, 4 AP/Wide World Photos; p. 5 AP/Wide World Photos

Unit 1 Opener: p. 13 Culver Pictures

Lesson 1: pp. 14, 15 Jericho Historical Society, Jericho, Vermont

Lesson 2: p. 22 the Granger Collection; p. 23 Corbis-Bettmann

Lesson 3: p. 30 AP/Wide World Photos; p. 31 Culver Pictures

Lesson 4: p. 38 UPI/Corbis-Bettmann; p. 39 AP/Wide World Photos

Lesson 5: p. 46 The Granger Collection; p. 47 Culver Pictures

Lesson 6: p. 54 Culver Pictures; p. 55 Brown Brothers

Lesson 7: p. 62 Fred Mae, Mission News Company; p. 63 San Francisco Public Library

Unit 2 Opener: p. 75 UPI/Corbis-Bettmann

Lesson 8: p. 76 AP/Wide World Photos; p. 77 Brown Brothers

Lesson 9: p. 84 from *Animals Are My Hobby* by Gertrude Davies Lintz, © 1942,
Robert M. McBride & Company; p. 85 Courtesy of the Zoological Society of Philadelphia

Lesson 10: pp. 92, 93 Brown Brothers

Lesson 11: pp. 100, 101 UPI/Corbis-Bettmann

Lesson 12: p. 108 The Granger Collection; p. 109 Michael J. Howell/Gamma-Liaison

Lesson 13: p. 116 Archive Photos; p. 117 Corbis-Bettmann

Lesson 14: p. 124 Deborah Feingold/Archive Photos; p. 125 NASA

Unit 3 Opener: p. 137 Amanda Feilding and Joseph Mullen

Lesson 15: p. 138 Corbis-Bettmann; p. 139 The Granger Collection

Lesson 16: p. 146 Culver Pictures; p. 147 Archive Photos

Lesson 17: p. 154 Erich Lessing/Art Resource, New York; p. 155 Scala/Art Resource, New York

Lesson 18: p. 162 Amanda Feilding and Joseph Mullen; p. 163 The Granger Collection

Lesson 19: pp. 170, 171 AP/Wide World Photos

Lesson 20: p. 178 Retuers/Steve Dipaola/Archive Photos; p. 179 AP/Wide World Photos

Lesson 21: p. 186 A. Hernandez/Sygma; p. 187 Les Stone/Sygma